MRCP PART 1 MCQs

With Key Topic Summaries

Second Edition

MRCP PART 1
MCQs

With Key
Topic Summaries

Second Edition

PAUL O'NEILL
BSc(Hons) MB ChB MD FRCP(UK)

Senior Lecturer in Geriatric Medicine,
Hospital Dean for Clinical Studies,
Curricular Facilitator,
Faculty of Medicine, Dentistry and Nursing,
University of Manchester

First Edition 1987
Second Edition 1997
Reprinted 2000, 2001, 2002

A catalogue record for this book is available from the British Library.

ISBN 1 901198 07 3

The information contained within this book was obtained by the author from reliable sources. However, while every effort has been made to ensure its accuracy, no responsibility for loss, damage or injury occasioned to any person acting or refraining from action as a result of information contained herein can be accepted by the publishers or authors.

PasTest Revision Books and Intensive Courses

PasTest has been established in the field of postgraduate medical education since 1972, providing revision books and intensive study courses for doctors preparing for their professional examinations. Books and courses are available for the following specialities: **MRCP Part 1 and 2, MRCPCH Part 1 and 2, MRCOG, DRCOG, MRCGP, DCH, FRCA, MRCS, PLAB.**
For further details contact:

PasTest, Freepost, Knutsford, Cheshire WA16 7BR
Tel: 01565 752000 Fax: 01565 650264

Text prepared and printed by MFP Design & Print, Longford Trading Estate, Thomas Street, Stretford, Manchester M32 0JT.

CONTENTS

MORE PASTEST BOOKS FOR MRCP PART 1 CANDIDATES

ESSENTIAL REVISION NOTES FOR MRCP: REVISED EDITION

Dr Kalra's unique best-seller has been thoroughly revised and updated to provide the definitive guide to revision for all MRCP candidates.

- Large format with over 650 pages
- A definitive guide to revision for the MRCP exam
- Concise presentation of information, hints and tips, unlike conventional textbooks
- Essential facts highlighted
- Invaluable revision checklists
- Diagrams, illustrations and bullet points to aid learning

Essential Revision Notes for MRCP: Revised edition, P Kalra, FRCP RCP Tutor, 2002, ISBN 1 901198 59 6. Ref: 1111. £34.95

MRCP PART 1 NEW 'BEST OF FIVE' MULTIPLE CHOICE REVISION BOOK

This new title reflects the new format of 'Best of Five' Multiple Choice Questions for paper 2 of the MRCP Part 1 examination.

- Over 300 new ëBest of fiveí questions with expanded explanations
- Subject-based chapters reflecting the actual exam content to test your knowledge and highlight weak areas for further revision
- Checklist of vital topics for effective revision

MRCP 1 New 'Best of five' Multiple Choice Revision Book, K Binymin, MBChB MRCP MSc, 2002 ISBN 1 901198 57 X. Ref: 1200. £19.95.

MRCP 1 MULTIPLE TRUE/FALSE REVISION BOOK

This new title available soon carefully reflects the content of the Royal College of Physicians examination. It is an essential tool to help candidates pass the Part 1 exam.

- Over 600 PasTest Multiple True/False questions to give candidates essential practice for Paper 1 of the MRCP Part 1 examination
- Chapters arranged by subject, reflecting the actual exam content to test candidates' knowledge and highlight weak areas for further revision
- Checklist of vital topics for effective revision

MRCP 1 Multiple True/False Revision Book, P Kalra, FRCP RCP tutor, 2002, ISBN 1 901198 95 2. Ref: 1201. £24.95.

Credit card hotline: 01565 752000

PasTest Ltd,
FREEPOST
Knutsford
WA16 7BR

Fax: +44 (0)1565 650264
www.pastest.co.uk

Please turn to page 183 for further titles.

INTRODUCTION *(you should read this!)*

This book is designed to help you prepare for the MRCP Part 1 by

- providing subject summaries rather than simply brief answers to each question
- concentrating mainly on the clinical sciences. Most candidates are very anxious about these questions. This book provides a framework for your revision.

Use the boxes provided against each question to mark your answer — T for True, F for False, or a blank if you do not know the answer. If you guess the answer, put a special mark next to the question so that when you turn to the answers you will be able to see whether you are good at guessing!

The balance of questions in the book reflects the relative importance of the subjects in the exam and focuses on favourite topics found in the papers over the last few years.

In 1993, the Royal Colleges decided that the candidates for MRCP could select to do either a paediatric or a general medicine paper with half of the questions, on core topics, common to each. Within this review, the content of the examination was revised. The amended examination regulations state:

'Increased emphasis will in future be given to basic science topics. Questions in both options may be set on relevant principles of cell, molecular and membrane biology and immunology, genetics, and biochemistry, as well as anatomical, physiological, microbiological and pharmacological topics.'

No doubt, as you read this, you will feel your anxiety levels increasing! You need to know what this means for studying; how many questions will there be in the exam on basic sciences; will you have to relearn the Krebs' cycle! When I talked to candidates after the changes were announced they expressed similar worries. These have not been reduced by the exams since 1993. Eventually, the Royal College placed an advert in the BMJ to explain the changes. In it, they said a number of things that are crucial to your understanding of their thinking (and your approach to revision). I have included some of their statements about the exam below (in italics).

Because of the information available about the exam and the experience of the last few years, it is now much easier to give advice about revision and how to approach the paper.

KEY POINTS ABOUT CLINICAL SCIENCES

* About 25% of questions will be from the clinical sciences. It follows that these represent 75 of the total marks; you cannot ignore them or you will fail.
* Most of these questions will be part of the core 30 questions common to both general medicine and paediatrics.
* The great majority of the topics will be based on the science underlying the clinical problems that you are seeing from day to day on the ward. RCP – *'it seems from letters and comments received that some candidates believe that the examination is now predominantly about basic science and not about clinical medicine. This is incorrect.'*
* The questions will mainly be about common problems and common knowledge. RCP – *'The examination is not a test of esoteric knowledge.'* You should study from standard textbooks of medicine.

WHAT APPROACH SHOULD YOU ADOPT?

* You should revise sections in medium sized textbooks that describe the RELEVANT basic science. These contain the great majority of what you need.

* Go over the clinical science questions in this book. Test your knowledge, then read through the summaries very carefully. They contain a lot of relevant material in a concise form.

* The basic science questions are set mainly on topics published in leading articles and editorials in general medical journals such as the *British Medical Journal, The Lancet* and the *New England Journal of Medicine.* Remember that the exam is set at least 1 year in advance – do not waste time reading last week's journals!

ACKNOWLEDGEMENTS

I would like to thank the following people for providing questions and subject summaries for this book:

S.G. Brear, C. Buchanan, K. Channer, S. Ellis, D. Martin,
F. McCrae, C. Short and R. Stevens.

There are usually 4–5 cardiology (vascular disease) questions in the exam. In the core section, the examiners still tend to emphasise clinical cardiology, common physical signs and pharmacology. Most exams will contain questions such as 'the causes of a loud first heart sound include' or 'a third heart sound is found in'. You should start your revision by making a list of these and summarising the key features of each.

Clinical science topics that you might consider include:

- Causes of giant a-waves in the JVP
- Causes of cannon waves
- Loud S1
- Reverse, wide fixed, and variable splitting of S2
- Causes of S3, S4
- Anatomy of the coronary arteries
- Valsalva manoeuvre
- Valvular stenosis and incompetence – explanations of clinical signs
- Common congenital heart disease (often a core topic)
- Causes of a prolonged QT interval
- ACE inhibitors (frequent question, could be considered as a pharmacology topic)
- Constrictive pericarditis (haemodynamic consequences).

1. In normal coronary artery anatomy

- ☐ A the circumflex coronary artery lies in the posterior atrioventricular groove
- ☐ B the right coronary artery supplies the superior and anterior portion of the interventricular septum
- ☐ C the circumflex coronary artery supplies the cardiac apex
- ☐ D the left anterior descending artery supplies the atrioventricular node
- ☐ E the obtuse marginal artery is a branch of the circumflex artery

2. **The following are useful in the investigation of a possible phaeochromocytoma:**

☐ A 24-hour urinary excretion of vanilmandelic acid (VMA)
☐ B whole body ^{131}I metaiodobenzylguanidine (MIBG) scan
☐ C pentolinium suppression test
☐ D computed tomography of abdomen and chest
☐ E 24-hour urinary excretion of 5 hydroxy indolacetic acid (5HIAA)

3. **The following are characteristic features of chronic constrictive pericarditis:**

☐ A enlarged heart on chest radiograph
☐ B atrial fibrillation
☐ C pericardial friction rub
☐ D reduction of the jugular venous pressure with inspiration
☐ E pulsus paradoxus

4. **Features of rejection of a heart transplant include**

☐ A pyrexia
☐ B prolongation of the PR interval
☐ C increase in cardiac size on chest radiograph
☐ D chest pain
☐ E reduction in the voltages of the QRS complex

5. **The following statements are correct:**

☐ A the normal pericardial fluid volume is 60–100 ml
☐ B the coronary sinus drains into the superior vena cava
☐ C the heart normally weighs 500 g
☐ D the transverse cardiac diameter is normally less than 50% of the transthoracic diameter
☐ E the right atrium normally indents the oesophagus

6.   In mitral stenosis

- ☐   A   a chest infection can precipitate left ventricular failure
- ☐   B   the chest radiograph may show narrowing of the carina
- ☐   C   atrial fibrillation always occurs
- ☐   D   the pulmonary wedge pressure is lower than the left ventricular end diastolic pressure
- ☐   E   mitral valvotomy is contraindicated in patients over 60 years of age

7.   The following are normal findings on an electrocardiograph:

- ☐   A   PR interval of 0.22 seconds
- ☐   B   mean frontal QRS axis – 40 degrees
- ☐   C   R wave in aVL of 12 mm
- ☐   D   right bundle branch block
- ☐   E   Q wave in lead III

8.   The following cardiological findings may be associated with thyroid disease:

- ☐   A   collapsing pulse
- ☐   B   pericardial effusion
- ☐   C   atrial fibrillation
- ☐   D   right bundle branch block
- ☐   E   hypertension

9.   In congenital heart disease

- ☐   A   ostium secundum atrial septal defects (ASD) lie adjacent to the atrioventricular valves
- ☐   B   the ECG may show a prolonged PR interval in ostium primum ASD
- ☐   C   ventricular septal defect (VSD) is the commonest congenital heart lesion
- ☐   D   osteogenesis imperfecta is associated with aortic incompetence
- ☐   E   the recurrence risk in siblings of affected children with VSD is 25%

10. The following circulatory changes occur in pregnancy:

☐ A   increase in cardiac output by 30%
☐ B   increase in heart rate by 30 beats/minute
☐ C   increase in systemic blood pressure
☐ D   decreased pulmonary vascular resistance
☐ E   increase in blood volume of 40%

11. In Fallot's tetralogy, cyanosis is increased

☐ A   by exercise
☐ B   by taking a hot bath
☐ C   by crying
☐ D   by squatting
☐ E   in the first few months of life

12. In the jugular venous pulse

☐ A   the a wave coincides with a fourth heart sound
☐ B   the c wave coincides with isometric contraction of the right ventricle
☐ C   a sustained rise of at least 1 cm will occur in normal individuals when the upper abdomen is compressed
☐ D   the x descent coincides with a third heart sound
☐ E   the v wave coincides with the upstroke of the carotid pulse

13. The following will be accentuated by prompt squatting from a standing position:

☐ A   the murmur of aortic regurgitation
☐ B   the fourth heart sound
☐ C   the murmur of ventricular septal defect in Eisenmenger's syndrome
☐ D   the systolic murmur associated with hypertrophic obstructive cardiomyopathy
☐ E   the interval between the first heart sound and the systolic click of mitral valve prolapse

14. The following would favour a ventricular rather than a supraventricular origin of a broad complex tachycardia:

- ☐ A varying intensity of the second heart sound
- ☐ B the presence of fusion beats
- ☐ C a right bundle branch block pattern
- ☐ D a mean frontal plane axis of +120°
- ☐ E QRS duration >140 ms

15. The Valsalva manoeuvre

- ☐ A causes a decrease in heart size
- ☐ B increases the murmur of aortic valvular stenosis
- ☐ C accentuates the delay between the first heart sound and the systolic click of mitral valve prolapse
- ☐ D leads to a decrease in intrathoracic pressure
- ☐ E diminishes the murmur of hypertrophic obstructive cardiomyopathy

16. Reversed splitting of the second heart sound occurs in

- ☐ A tetralogy of Fallot
- ☐ B left bundle branch block (LBBB)
- ☐ C patent ductus arteriosus (PDA)
- ☐ D mitral regurgitation
- ☐ E aortic stenosis

17. The following are true of infective endocarditis:

- ☐ A *Streptococcus viridans* is the most common organism affecting prosthetic valves
- ☐ B the predisposing risk is greater in mitral stenosis than in mitral regurgitation
- ☐ C polymicrobial infection occurs in 5% of patients
- ☐ D *Staphylococcus aureus* rarely affects previously abnormal valves
- ☐ E patients may have no heart murmur at presentation

18. Nitric oxide

☐ A   antagonises the vasodilatory effect of prostacyclin
☐ B   is released from macrophages
☐ C   causes platelet disaggregation
☐ D   causes an increase in cAMP
☐ E   is depleted by nitrates

19. In a patient prescribed a selective alpha-blocking drug, the following may occur:

☐ A   postural hypotension with a tachycardia
☐ B   improvement in prostatic symptoms
☐ C   reduction of LDL with prolonged therapy
☐ D   increased plasma glucose with prolonged therapy
☐ E   reduction in left ventricular mass with prolonged therapy

20. The following are true of physiological murmurs:

☐ A   changes in posture and exercise characteristically alter the intensity of the murmur
☐ B   they are usually of low intensity
☐ C   they are most frequently heard in diastole
☐ D   they may be continuous
☐ E   they are frequently heard in older patients

CLINICAL PHARMACOLOGY

Most people feel that there are a lot of 'drug' questions in the exam, and their reactions to this are affected by how difficult they perceive the questions to be! It is true that there are often 5–6 questions centred around drugs and most of these are found in the core (overlap) section. However, the College's classification is based on:

* 1 question on toxicology
* 1–2 questions on 'clinical pharmacology'
* 3+ questions on 'systems' or organ based pharmacology.

You need to structure your work accordingly.

Common topics that you should revise include:

* Poisoning – you cannot cover all the possible things that people take. You have to concentrate on the common ones. These include salicylate, paracetamol, tricyclic antidepressants and lithium. Frequently, the College asks questions that cover more than one drug such as: 'The following are true of drug overdose…'.
* Drug interactions appear on most papers, frequently related to anticoagulants, digoxin, hypoglycaemics, amiodarone and antiepileptics.
* Each of these drugs is an important topic in its own right and you *must* spend time revising them. Other topics include sulphasalazine and thiazides.
* You should consider alterations in pharmacokinetics – prescribing in renal failure, first pass effect.
* Questions on drugs and pregnancy frequently occur, including contraindications in breast feeding. Such questions are not confined to the paediatric section.
* You should be aware of the common teratogenic effects.
* You should cover systems based pharmacology when you are revising that particular organ system. Examples would be drugs and the kidney (interstitial nephritis) or the lung (pulmonary fibrosis).
* It is also worth revising a little about drugs and the skin (for example photosensitivity).
* Remember, when answering questions about drugs, it is safer to say something does occur, rather than being confident that it does not.

21. Induction of vomiting

☐ A is solely dependent on dopamine receptor activation
☐ B can be carried out by stimulation of the chemoreceptor trigger zone in the third ventricle
☐ C is prevented by the anticholinergic effect of metoclopramide
☐ D can be reduced after cytotoxic chemotherapy by ondansetron
☐ E is prevented by domperidone acting directly on the emetic centre in the medulla

22. In patients receiving lithium therapy

☐ A the aim should be to produce a serum level of less than 2.5 mmol/l
☐ B altered bowel habit is an absolute indication for cessation of therapy
☐ C ECG and EEG changes occur only in the toxic range
☐ D polyuria and chronic renal toxicity are related to the dosage used in the long term
☐ E breast feeding is contraindicated

23. In patients with renal impairment

☐ A all tetracyclines are contraindicated
☐ B if diabetic, the insulin requirement usually falls
☐ C nitrofurantoin is of value in the treatment of urinary infections
☐ D ethambutol can be safely given
☐ E potassium sparing diuretics are often required in those patients receiving high dose frusemide

24. The following statements are correct:

☐ A aspirin in a dose of 75 mg is proven to reduce the risk of stroke
☐ B there is no difference in gastrointestinal bleeding rates between 75 mg and 325 mg of aspirin per day
☐ C the action of aspirin is dependent on the irreversible inhibition of lipoxygenase in the platelet
☐ D prostacyclin production is reduced by aspirin
☐ E the restoration of thromboxane production after aspirin requires the release of new platelets

25. The following are true with regard to anticonvulsant drugs:

☐ A   the plasma therapeutic range refers to free drug concentration
☐ B   the relationship of the dose to plasma concentration for phenytoin is linear
☐ C   lamotrigine exerts its anticonvulsant effects through increasing GABA levels
☐ D   the anticonvulsant effect of sodium valproate at any given time is directly related to the plasma concentration
☐ E   diazepam and phenytoin are poorly absorbed from the intramuscular route

26. In the treatment of schizophrenia

☐ A   haloperidol has a greater incidence of extra-pyramidal side-effects than chlorpromazine
☐ B   weight loss is often a significant problem
☐ C   the neuroleptic drugs exert their antipsychotic effects by blocking dopamine transmission
☐ D   after two years the relapse rate on treatment is no different from that on placebo
☐ E   the addition of lithium may be useful in chronic schizophrenia

27. In malignant hyperpyrexia

☐ A   the diagnosis may be made by exposing muscle *in vitro* to tubocurarine
☐ B   premedication with diazepam is safe
☐ C   suxamethonium is contraindicated as a muscle relaxant
☐ D   thiopentone may be safely used
☐ E   dantrolene sodium may be useful in the treatment

28. The following drugs can cause hepatic damage:

☐ A   streptomycin
☐ B   ethambutol
☐ C   rifampicin
☐ D   pyrazinamide
☐ E   isoniazid

29. The following drugs may cause a toxic retinopathy:

☐ A thioridazine
☐ B chloroquine
☐ C ethambutol
☐ D frusemide
☐ E amiodarone

30. The following drugs have been implicated in acute interstitial nephritis:

☐ A benzyl penicillin
☐ B phenytoin
☐ C tetracycline
☐ D streptomycin
☐ E bendrofluazide

31. In elderly people

☐ A glomerular filtration rate starts to decline rapidly after the age of 70 years
☐ B lean body mass is the same at 80 years as it is at 40 years
☐ C protein binding of drugs declines with age
☐ D the cardiovascular response to propranolol increases with age
☐ E the rate of hepatic drug metabolism declines with age

32. In pregnancy

☐ A the volume of distribution of drugs is unchanged
☐ B plasma protein binding of drugs increases
☐ C hepatic metabolism of drugs is unchanged
☐ D renal elimination of ampicillin is increased
☐ E ingested medications may be metabolised in the fetal liver

33. The following are true of the benzodiazepines:

- [ ] A the half life of diazepam is four times longer at the age of 80 years than it is at 20 years of age in normal individuals
- [ ] B diazepam is metabolised to desmethyl diazepam which has similar properties but a half life of 50–120 hours
- [ ] C the retention of the glucuronide metabolites of lorazepam and oxazepam requires the dose to be reduced in renal failure
- [ ] D the receptor density is greatest in the neocortex, hippocampus and cerebellum
- [ ] E the excretion of diazepam is unaltered in cirrhosis

34. After overdose with digoxin

- [ ] A hypokalaemia is common
- [ ] B xanthopsia occurs
- [ ] C abdominal pain and diarrhoea occur
- [ ] D confusion is common in elderly people
- [ ] E sinus bradycardia with first degree heart block is commonly found

35. A patient in casualty has a salicylate level of 520 mg/l, 12 hours after taking an overdose

- [ ] A the treatment of choice is forced alkaline diuresis
- [ ] B N-acetyl-cysteine should be administered
- [ ] C vitamin K_1 should be administered
- [ ] D a chest radiograph may show pulmonary oedema
- [ ] E a good prognostic sign is the presence of clear consciousness

36. **The following are true of the angiotensin-converting enzyme inhibitors:**

☐ A enalapril is a pro-drug
☐ B if hypotension occurs after the first dose of enalapril it is usually within 1 hour
☐ C potassium-sparing diuretics are a useful adjunct to treatment
☐ D they are indicated in the management of hypertension secondary to bilateral renal artery stenosis
☐ E captopril is associated with the nephrotic syndrome

37. **The following poisons are correctly linked with their specific antidote:**

☐ A arsenic – dimercaprol
☐ B suxamethonium – neostigmine
☐ C organophosphates – thiosulphate
☐ D methanol – ethanol
☐ E thallium – Prussian blue

38. **The following drugs owe their effect to interference with folate metabolism:**

☐ A trimethoprim
☐ B pyrimethamine
☐ C sulphadimidine
☐ D methotrexate
☐ E cephalexin

39. **In the Vaughan-Williams classification of anti-arrhythmic drugs**

☐ A class 1c drugs prolong the cardiac action potential
☐ B class 3 drugs act chiefly on slow calcium channels
☐ C class 4 drugs are beta-blockers
☐ D class 1b drugs predispose to Torsade de Pointes type ventricular arrhythmias
☐ E amiodarone has effects in classes 1, 2, 3 and 4

40. Adenosine

- ☐ A is competitively inhibited by disopyramide
- ☐ B has a stimulatory effect on the atrioventricular node which is mediated by calcium channel blockade
- ☐ C is a naturally occurring purine nucleotide
- ☐ D has a half life of less than 1 minute
- ☐ E increases the atrial rate in atrial fibrillation

41. In treatment with gentamicin

- ☐ A the dose interval is calculated from the trough level
- ☐ B if treatment continues over 2 weeks, nephrotoxicity and ototoxicity can occur even if the levels are therapeutic
- ☐ C the peak level should be kept between 4–10 µg/ml
- ☐ D renal toxicity is increased in combination with frusemide
- ☐ E if the trough level is high and the peak level is acceptable, then the individual dose should be reduced

42. Non-steroidal anti-inflammatory drugs

- ☐ A work by inhibiting lipoxygenase
- ☐ B can reduce the chronic cough of captopril
- ☐ C can cause an aseptic meningitis in SLE
- ☐ D are more effective in osteoarthrosis than paracetamol
- ☐ E enhance the antihypertensive effect of beta-blockers

43. In the treatment of breast carcinoma with tamoxifen

- ☐ A oestrogen receptor negative tumours may respond
- ☐ B the drug has a short half life
- ☐ C a rapid response is often seen
- ☐ D hypocalcaemia may be found in the initial stages
- ☐ E response is as frequent in pre- as in post-menopausal women

44. Medical factors considered in the use of the oral contraceptive pill include

☐ A progesterone only preparations increase the blood pressure
☐ B a previous history of arterial or venous thrombosis is a contraindication for a progesterone only pill
☐ C combined preparations should be avoided in sickle cell disease
☐ D malignant melanomas may be oestrogen dependent
☐ E the progesterone only pill is preferred in epilepsy

45. Warfarin

☐ A reduces vitamin K dependent clotting factors
☐ B reacts with ampicillin to increase anticoagulant effect
☐ C appears in breast milk in quantities too small to affect the baby
☐ D has an increased anticoagulant effect with griseofulvin therapy
☐ E has significant antifibrinolytic therapy

There are usually 4–5 questions in the exam on respiratory medicine. Frequently, these are based on pulmonary physiology. Unlike cardiology, it is unusual to have any questions on physical signs. Common topics that you should cover include:

- Increased and decreased transfer factor
- Hypoxia
- Hypercarbia, hypocarbia (hyperventilation)
- Acid base disturbance (could be considered under metabolic medicine – a very important topic)
- Normal pulmonary physiology (you have to understand this to answer many questions on deranged physiology)
- Oxygen dissociation curve and shifts
- Respiratory failure (combination of topics from above)
- Physiological effects of long term oxygen therapy
- Pathophysiological effects (and clinical symptoms, signs, aetiology) of sleep apnoea syndrome

46. The following may cause an increase in transfer factor:

☐ A athletic training
☐ B emphysema
☐ C VSD with right to left shunt
☐ D polycythaemia
☐ E pulmonary haemorrhage

47. The following reduce total pulmonary compliance:

☐ A fibrosing alveolitis
☐ B emphysema
☐ C mitral stenosis of long standing
☐ D ankylosing spondylitis
☐ E acute respiratory distress syndrome (ARDS)

48. The oxygen–haemoglobin dissociation curve is displaced to the right by

☐ A   an increase in hydrogen ion concentration
☐ B   an increase in PCO_2
☐ C   a fall in temperature
☐ D   increased lactate production
☐ E   chronic hypoxia due to cyanotic heart disease

49. The following statements are correct:

☐ A   there is 50% greater resistance to breathing when breathing via the nose
☐ B   the main carina is normally fixed with no significant movement with respiration
☐ C   in the supine position, there is a greater tendency to aspirate into the upper rather than the lower lobes
☐ D   total airways resistance is greater in the small airways than in the trachea
☐ E   type I pneumocytes secrete and store surfactant

50. The following diseases are characterised by a rise in $PaCO_2$:

☐ A   emphysema
☐ B   respiratory involvement in Guillain–Barré syndrome
☐ C   chronic bronchitis
☐ D   fibrosing alveolitis
☐ E   pulmonary embolus

51. In the sleep apnoea syndrome

☐ A   the patients are usually thin
☐ B   pulmonary hypertension is a prominent feature
☐ C   a rise in daytime PCO_2 is unusual
☐ D   progesterone may be used in treatment
☐ E   night sedation is a useful therapeutic measure

52. The following are recognised pulmonary complications of acquired immune deficiency syndrome (AIDS):

☐ A *Pneumocystis carinii* pneumonia
☐ B Kaposi's sarcoma
☐ C pulmonary veno-occlusive disease
☐ D cytomegalovirus pneumonia
☐ E atypical mycobacterial infections

53. In bronchoalveolar lavage fluid

☐ A the finding of asbestos bodies is diagnostic of asbestosis
☐ B sarcoidosis is characterised by a preponderance of polymorphs
☐ C there is an increase in total cell count in smokers
☐ D non-smokers have proportionately more macrophages and polymorphs
☐ E the findings in sarcoidosis are a better guide to the diagnosis than bronchial and transbronchial biopsy

54. The following features suggest that a carcinoma of the left main bronchus is probably inoperable:

☐ A a FEV_1 of 1.3 litres
☐ B a right recurrent laryngeal nerve palsy
☐ C a wide, fixed carina at bronchoscopy
☐ D tumour within 1 cm of the main carina
☐ E hypercalcaemia with squamous cell carcinoma

55. The following are true of α_1 anti-trypsin deficiency:

☐ A it is much more common in men
☐ B it tends to cause emphysema more marked at the lung apices
☐ C prognosis is unaffected by smoking
☐ D levels of α_1 anti-trypsin may fall within the normal ranges
☐ E an MM phenotype is found within the normal population

56. In fibrosing alveolitis

- [ ] A cough is an uncommon symptom
- [ ] B polyarthralgia occurs in a significant minority of patients
- [ ] C clubbing of the fingers occurs in virtually all patients
- [ ] D antinuclear factor (ANF) is positive in up to half of patients
- [ ] E there may be an associated Sjögren's syndrome

57. The following are true of extrinsic allergic alveolitis:

- [ ] A it only occurs in atopic individuals
- [ ] B it can be caused by psittacosis
- [ ] C it characteristically causes an eosinophilia
- [ ] D farmer's lung is often associated with precipitins to thermophilic actinomyces in blood
- [ ] E it is associated with fever in the acute phase

58. The following are true with regard to *Aspergillus* related diseases:

- [ ] A aspergilloma is usually associated with peripheral blood eosinophilia
- [ ] B they may be associated with bronchocentric granulomatosis
- [ ] C only a minority of patients with allergic bronchopulmonary aspergillosis have positive *Aspergillus* precipitins
- [ ] D high dose Septrin is the treatment of choice in invasive aspergillosis
- [ ] E bronchiectasis is a common complication of allergic bronchopulmonary aspergillosis

59. The following are true of Legionnaires' disease:

- [ ] A drinking contaminated water is the commonest cause of the disease
- [ ] B high concentrations of the organism may be released from a contaminated tap when first used in the morning
- [ ] C abdominal pain and diarrhoea are frequent
- [ ] D microscopic haematuria is common
- [ ] E diagnosis is most frequently made by isolation of the organism from blood cultures

60. The following treatments are matched with appropriate complications:

☐ A isoniazid may cause peripheral neuropathy
☐ B ethambutol causes jaundice
☐ C disseminated Bacillus-Calmette-Guérin (BCG) infection often occurs in atopic individuals
☐ D rifampicin causes orange urine
☐ E pyrazinamide causes hepatic toxicity

61. The following are true of spontaneous pneumothorax:

☐ A it is associated with Ehlers–Danlos syndrome
☐ B it may be associated with auscultatory clicks
☐ C it is associated with positive end expiratory pressure (PEEP) during intermittent positive pressure ventilation (IPPV)
☐ D it causes an obstructive defect on pulmonary function
☐ E it may occur in tuberculosis

62. The following are indications for the mandatory use of steroids in sarcoidosis:

☐ A bilateral hilar lymphadenopathy
☐ B ocular involvement
☐ C erythema nodosum
☐ D cerebral involvement
☐ E arthralgia

63. The following are true of the normal radiograph:

☐ A it is abnormal for the hemidiaphragms to be at the same height on a routine inspiratory film
☐ B on a normal inspiratory film the right diaphragm is at the level of the anterior end of the 9th rib
☐ C the trachea is often slightly deviated to the right
☐ D the heart size varies about 1 cm between diastole and systole
☐ E the main carina occurs at the level of the 4th–5th thoracic vertebra in a routine PA film

64. Occupational exposure to the following materials may cause the diseases listed:

☐ A asbestos causes peritoneal mesothelioma
☐ B coal workers may develop progressive massive fibrosis
☐ C fibreglass inhalation causes bronchial carcinoma
☐ D isocyanates cause asthma
☐ E tin oxide dust causes severe pulmonary fibrosis

65. Pulmonary hypertension

☐ A is suggested by a mean pulmonary artery pressure of 12 mm Hg
☐ B may be caused by schistosomiasis
☐ C is associated with gross obesity
☐ D in Great Britain, is most commonly caused by recurrent pulmonary embolism
☐ E in its primary form can usually be distinguished from recurrent pulmonary emboli at cardiac catheterisation

Candidates often do very poorly in neurology questions. This is because of several factors: lack of teaching at medical school, insufficient experience post-qualification, and insecurity about neurological knowledge leading to a low response rate to multiple choice questions. Some of these factors are difficult to correct, but it is possible to gain reasonable marks in the exam providing you are aware of the favourite topics.

There are generally 6 questions in the exam on neurological topics. At least half of these will be on neuroanatomical knowledge with the remainder often requiring some awareness of neurological basic science. You must spend time learning the anatomical pathways, it is not something you can work out on the day (looking at your hand will not reveal the course of the median nerve!).

Topics that you must cover include:
• Anatomy (and lesions) of the cranial nerves – this appears on most papers
• Anatomy (and lesions) of peripheral nerves (in particular the hands)
• Anatomy of spinal cord (and the consequences of damage)
• Mechanisms of treatment of Parkinson's disease
• Motor neurone lesions (upper/motor/combined)
• Consequences of damage to cerebral circulation (more common recently)

66. The following are true of the posterior columns of the spinal cord:

☐ A fibres originate in the cuneate and gracilis nuclei
☐ B blood supply is derived from a spinal artery entering around T_{12}
☐ C light touch is transmitted
☐ D it is mainly composed of small myelinated and unmyelinated fibres
☐ E damage may induce pseudo-athetosis

67. In a patient with hearing problems

☐ A loudness recruitment is found in Ménière's syndrome
☐ B tone decay is found in acoustic neuromas
☐ C in an acoustic neuroma, bone conduction will be greater than air conduction
☐ D the lesion may be in the two cochlear nuclei
☐ E the lesion may be in fibres projecting to the medial geniculate nucleus

68. The following muscles are supplied by the lateral popliteal nerve:

☐ A tibialis anterior
☐ B extensor hallucis longus
☐ C soleus and peroneals
☐ D extensor digitorum longus
☐ E flexor digitorum brevis

69. The following statements are true:

☐ A Betz's cells are found in the post-central gyrus of the cerebral cortex
☐ B Purkinje cells are found in the basal ganglia
☐ C the vagus nerve is predominantly composed of unmyelinated 'C' fibres
☐ D gamma motor neurones are involved in the clasp knife response
☐ E vertical gaze is controlled by nuclei situated in the midbrain

70. The following are true of muscle spindles and their connections:

☐ A increased activity from gamma motor neurones leads to cog-wheel rigidity
☐ B increased firing of the fusimotor fibres causes an increased tone
☐ C afferent fibres are found in the dorsal root of the spinal cord
☐ D Golgi tendon receptors protect against excessive stretch
☐ E they are involved in the cremasteric reflex

71. In the control of bladder function

☐ A increased detrusor muscle activity leads to urinary retention
☐ B alpha-adrenergic receptors are located within the trigone
☐ C outflow from the sacral portion of the spinal cord is predominantly sympathetic
☐ D the nerve supply is derived from the external pudendal nerve
☐ E cholinergic stimulation lowers bladder wall tone

72. The trigeminal nerve

☐ A   originates in the floor of the 4th ventricle
☐ B   has fibres carrying light touch which project to the cervical spinal cord
☐ C   has motor fibres which are equally distributed through the maxillary and mandibular branches
☐ D   supplies sensation over the vertex
☐ E   involvement in a central lesion initially causes loss of sensation near the angle of the jaw

73. Dopaminergic pathways

☐ A   are found within the neocortex
☐ B   have a predominantly excitatory function
☐ C   originate in the basal ganglia
☐ D   are the main system affected in Alzheimer's disease
☐ E   when stimulated release dopamine which is broken down by monoamine oxidase type B

74. The following are true of substance P:

☐ A   it is found mainly within the cerebral cortex
☐ B   its main function is pain modulation
☐ C   the major action is as an inhibitory neurotransmitter
☐ D   the structure resembles 5-hydroxytryptamine
☐ E   sodium valproate mimics its actions

75. In the treatment of spasticity

☐ A   baclofen will reduce tone without producing weakness
☐ B   an advantage of the use of baclofen is high penetration into the CSF
☐ C   diazepam is useful in patients with spinal cord transections
☐ D   dantrolene sodium inhibits the actions of glycine within the spinal cord
☐ E   injections of phenol may be of benefit

76. In nystagmus

☐ A the patient may be aware of the visual movement
☐ B the abducting eye fails to move completely in ataxic nystagmus
☐ C if the direction is downwards, the lesion is around the foramen magnum
☐ D upwards and downwards nystagmus are seen in benign positional vertigo
☐ E in a right cerebellar lesion, nystagmus will be maximal on looking to the left

77. If a patient has normal pressure hydrocephalus

☐ A insertion of a ventriculo-peritoneal shunt is of definite benefit in most patients
☐ B extrapyramidal features may be present
☐ C the duration of symptoms is a good guide to response to treatment
☐ D dementia is almost always present
☐ E measurements made on a CT scan can predict the response to insertion of a shunt

78. In patients with carotid stenosis of 80% and a recent transient ischaemic attack in that territory

☐ A a bruit will be present in the majority with gross narrowing
☐ B the annual risk of stroke will be over 25%
☐ C the risk from an operation will be <1% in most centres
☐ D an endarterectomy is superior to medical treatment in preventing strokes
☐ E altitudinous hemianopia may occur on the contralateral side to the symptomatic artery

79. In patients with a subarachnoid haemorrhage

☐ A blood will be seen within the CSF spaces in the majority of cases
☐ B the risk of developing a hydrocephalus is small
☐ C a major cause of morbidity is vasospasm
☐ D it may present as a third cranial nerve palsy in aneurysm of the anterior communicating artery
☐ E angiography almost always localises the site of the bleeding

80. The following statements are true:

- ☐ A in a brainstem stroke the patient may look towards the hemiparetic side
- ☐ B when the eye is abducted the superior oblique muscle acts as a pure depressor
- ☐ C in progressive supranuclear palsy involuntary fixation may be un-impaired
- ☐ D downward gaze is severely affected in progressive supranuclear palsy
- ☐ E upward gaze may be affected in Parkinson's disease

81. An oligoclonal band may appear in the cerebrospinal fluid in

- ☐ A systemic lupus erythematosus
- ☐ B sarcoidosis
- ☐ C tumours
- ☐ D multiple myeloma
- ☐ E subacute sclerosing panencephalitis

82. In multiple sclerosis

- ☐ A onset after the age of 40 years indicates a better prognosis
- ☐ B magnetic resonance imaging may be useful in confirming the diagnosis
- ☐ C initial presentation with motor symptoms indicates a better prognosis
- ☐ D a homonymous hemianopia is a common feature
- ☐ E red–green colour vision may be impaired

83. In a patient with subacute combined degeneration of the spinal cord

- ☐ A megaloblastic anaemia is always present
- ☐ B the dorsal root ganglia are severely affected
- ☐ C dementia is a common complication
- ☐ D fever may occur
- ☐ E the plantar response may be absent

84. In the upper limb

☐ A   the posterior interosseus nerve supplies abductor pollicis longus
☐ B   the root supply of opponens pollicis is T1
☐ C   supinator is supplied by the radial nerve
☐ D   pronator teres is supplied by the radial nerve
☐ E   the palmar interossei are innervated by the ulnar nerve

85. In the differential diagnosis of dementia

☐ A   a multi-infarct aetiology is more common than the Alzheimer's type
☐ B   a CT scan will reliably distinguish between Alzheimer's and multi-infarct dementia
☐ C   in Alzheimer's disease a gait disorder is seen at an early stage
☐ D   in Pick's disease severe memory loss is often found at an early stage
☐ E   in Jakob-Creutzfeldt disease an EEG may be characteristic

86. Muscle fasciculation occurs in

☐ A   cervical spondylosis
☐ B   lithium therapy
☐ C   Parkinson's disease
☐ D   Huntington's chorea
☐ E   hypomagnesaemia

87. The following are correct:

☐ A   an infarct in the anterior limb of the internal capsule causes sensory loss
☐ B   acalculia is a feature of Gerstmann's syndrome
☐ C   a parietal lobe lesion may cause left–right disorientation
☐ D   a frontal infarct may be asymptomatic
☐ E   a left occipital infarct causes a quadrantic right hemianopia

88. Cerebrospinal fluid

- [ ] A is absorbed by the arachnoid granulations
- [ ] B is produced only in the lateral ventricles
- [ ] C normally contains polymorphs
- [ ] D circulates directly between the third ventricle and the subarachnoid space
- [ ] E has a higher protein level in the ventricles than in the lumbar region

89. A neuronal action potential

- [ ] A is an all-or-none response
- [ ] B is produced by hyperpolarisation
- [ ] C produces an influx of potassium ions
- [ ] D makes the inside of the cell negative
- [ ] E propagates bidirectionally

There are usually 3–4 questions on endocrinology in the exam. At least 2 of them will be on clinical science relating to normal function (e.g. the following are true of cortisol). The other questions may test knowledge of abnormal function. You will find that most of what you need to know is contained in the chapters in the medium sized textbooks of medicine.

Important topics include:
* Insulin and ACTH
* Thyroxine and thyroid control
* Pituitary hormones
* Aldosterone
* FSH, LH, releasing factors
* Oestrogen and testosterone (including puberty)

90. Concerning Addison's disease

☐ A   the diagnosis can be excluded if serum cortisol is normal
☐ B   postural hypotension is often a feature
☐ C   blood urea concentration is usually low
☐ D   weight loss is an unusual feature
☐ E   its incidence is approximately 50% that of thyrotoxicosis

91. In thyrotoxicosis

☐ A   serum thyroxine concentration may be normal
☐ B   gynaecomastia may occur
☐ C   high serum TSH is responsible for the thyroid overactivity associated with Graves' disease
☐ D   the patient may be lethargic and depressed
☐ E   serum reverse triiodothyronine (T_3) level is usually reduced

92. The following statements are true of thyroid carcinoma:

☐ A   the most common histological type is anaplastic carcinoma
☐ B   it is rarely associated with hyperthyroidism
☐ C   previous neck irradiation in childhood may predispose to thyroid carcinoma in adult life
☐ D   medullary thyroid carcinoma may present with hypocalcaemia due to increased circulating calcitonin concentration
☐ E   it never occurs before puberty

93. Bromocriptine

☐ A   inhibits dopaminergic receptors
☐ B   stimulates prolactin secretion in normal subjects
☐ C   will suppress puerperal lactation
☐ D   suppresses growth hormone secretion in both normal subjects and acromegalics
☐ E   the commonest side-effect is palpitations

94. Phaeochromocytoma

☐ A   may be familial
☐ B   is rarely malignant
☐ C   may cause sustained rather than episodic hypertension
☐ D   may cause hyperthyroidism
☐ E   is associated with neurofibromatosis

95. In Cushing's syndrome associated with bronchial carcinoma

☐ A   the cause is secretion of corticosteroids by the tumour
☐ B   the classical physical findings are usually very florid
☐ C   24-hour urinary free cortisol excretion is not usually suppressed by dexamethasone administration
☐ D   hypokalaemia is more common than in patients with Cushing's syndrome from other causes
☐ E   the plasma ACTH level is not usually as high as in patients with pituitary-dependent Cushing's syndrome (Cushing's disease)

96. In acromegaly

☐ A   a high random serum growth hormone level confirms the diagnosis
☐ B   hypophosphataemia is a feature
☐ C   a reduced somatomedin C concentration usually occurs
☐ D   the cause may be a bronchial carcinoid tumour
☐ E   untreated patients may expect a normal life span

97. Hyperprolactinaemia in the female

☐ A   does not usually disturb the menstrual cycle
☐ B   may be caused by renal failure
☐ C   may be caused by metoclopramide
☐ D   is usually associated with an expanded pituitary fossa on lateral skull radiograph
☐ E   may cause decreased bone density

98. The following statements concerning gynaecomastia are true:

☐ A   it is usually due to an imbalance in the ratio of circulating androgen : oestrogen concentrations
☐ B   it is a common clinical presentation in the male with hyperprolactinaemia
☐ C   it may complicate treatment with spironolactone
☐ D   in a man with hypogonadotrophic hypogonadism, it is likely to be due to Klinefelter's syndrome
☐ E   in the majority of pubertal boys, it will require surgical correction (sub-areolar mastectomy)

99. The following are true of puberty:

☐ A   in normal girls the pubertal growth spurt precedes the menarche
☐ B   the first sign of puberty in the male is development of pubic hair
☐ C   precocious puberty is more likely to have a sinister underlying cause in a girl than in a boy
☐ D   the major action of cyproterone acetate is to suppress the secretion of growth hormone
☐ E   delayed pubertal development is most commonly due to a structural defect causing gonadotrophin deficiency

100. The following may occur in hypothyroidism:

☐ A   galactorrhoea
☐ B   carpal tunnel syndrome
☐ C   pretibial myxoedema
☐ D   macrocytosis
☐ E   a normal serum triiodothyronine (T_3) concentration

101. Concerning thyroiditis

☐ A   Hashimoto's thyroiditis is usually associated with a high titre of thyroid stimulating immunoglobulins
☐ B   subacute thyroiditis is believed to be viral in aetiology
☐ C   painful enlargement of the thyroid, a raised ESR and an increased radio-iodine uptake are consistent with a diagnosis of subacute thyroiditis
☐ D   there is an increased incidence of Hashimoto's thyroiditis in girls with Turner's syndrome
☐ E   the majority of patients with subacute thyroiditis will eventually develop permanent hypothyroidism

102. The following are true:

☐ A   the prostate can manufacture testosterone
☐ B   the testes produce about 50% of circulating testosterone
☐ C   testosterone is produced by Leydig cells in response to follicular stimulating hormone
☐ D   cyproterone acetate is a synthetic oestrogen
☐ E   gonadotrophin releasing hormone analogues stimulate luteinizing hormone reduction

103. TSH

☐ A   is a glycoprotein
☐ B   release is inhibited by metoclopropamide
☐ C   shares a common α-peptide chain with human chorionic gonadotrophin
☐ D   causes a reduction in cAMP
☐ E   acts on a specific cell membrane receptor

METABOLIC MEDICINE

You may want to deal with metabolic medicine alongside endocrinology; together there will probably be around 5 questions. Most papers contain questions on electrolyte or acid-base disturbance. You also need to cover diabetes mellitus and hypoglycaemia.

- Control of calcium - Vitamin D, parathormone, calcitonin
- Gluconeogenesis
- Mechanisms leading to hypoglycaemia
- ADH (SIADH)
- Electrolyte disturbance – hyper/hyponatraemia, hyper/hypokalaemia, hyper/hypocalcaemia
- Acid-base disturbance (also covered in respiratory medicine)
- Urate metabolism and excretion

104. The following are true of diabetes mellitus:

- ☐ A   chlorpropamide therapy may cause a low serum sodium
- ☐ B   it may be complicated by Charcot's joints
- ☐ C   it is associated with vitiligo
- ☐ D   necrobiosis lipoidica diabeticorum commonly affects the neck region
- ☐ E   the major disadvantage of human insulin is the high incidence of antibody formation compared with porcine and bovine insulin

105. The following may cause hypercalcaemia:

- ☐ A   secondary hyperparathyroidism
- ☐ B   pseudohypoparathyroidism
- ☐ C   vitamin D intoxication
- ☐ D   thyrotoxicosis
- ☐ E   Addison's disease

106. Hypoglycaemia may occur in

- ☐ A   patients receiving metformin
- ☐ B   liver disease
- ☐ C   Addison's disease
- ☐ D   multiple endocrine adenomatosis type 1
- ☐ E   patients receiving tolbutamide

107. Hypokalaemia is a feature of

- ☐ A   Cushing's syndrome
- ☐ B   Bartter's syndrome
- ☐ C   Conn's syndrome
- ☐ D   hyporeninaemic hypoaldosteronism
- ☐ E   Addison's disease

108. Metabolic acidosis

- ☐ A   is characterised by a low blood pH and a high plasma bicarbonate concentration
- ☐ B   will have a decreased PCO_2 if it is a simple metabolic acidosis
- ☐ C   will exhibit a normal anion gap if due to gastrointestinal alkali loss
- ☐ D   will exhibit an increased anion gap if due to lactic acidosis
- ☐ E   is always an indication for bicarbonate therapy

109. The following statements are true of hypermagnesaemia:

- ☐ A   symptomatic hypermagnesaemia is usually iatrogenic
- ☐ B   hypothyroidism may cause hypermagnesaemia
- ☐ C   symptoms are predominantly those of neuromuscular irritability
- ☐ D   it is usually accompanied by hypocalcaemia
- ☐ E   myoclonic jerks are frequently seen

110. In the control of parathormone secretion

- ☐ A   the C terminal fragment is biologically inactive
- ☐ B   the large precursor is cleaved by the Kupffer's cells in the liver
- ☐ C   chronic magnesium depletion stimulates parathormone production
- ☐ D   1,25 hydroxyvitamin D stimulates parathormone secretion
- ☐ E   parathormone stimulates 1,25 hydroxyvitamin D production

111. Atrial receptors

- [ ] A when stretched produce an increase in ADH release
- [ ] B if stimulated cause retention of sodium and water
- [ ] C stretching suppresses aldosterone and renin secretion
- [ ] D afferent fibres project through the phrenic nerve
- [ ] E stimulation causes a reflex with the efferent limb being mediated through the vagus nerve

112. In fat absorption and metabolism

- [ ] A chylomicrons are mostly composed of cholesterol
- [ ] B the reticuloendothelial system clears the chylomicron remnants
- [ ] C low density lipoproteins are cholesterol rich
- [ ] D cholesterol may be manufactured in many different cells
- [ ] E binding to apoprotein E regulates the transport of low density lipoproteins into cells

113. In potassium homeostasis

- [ ] A the normal daily intake is approximately equal to 50 mmol
- [ ] B in deficient states the kidney excretes approximately 15 mmol/l of potassium in the urine
- [ ] C in the colon and rectum potassium is reabsorbed
- [ ] D a total body deficit of 200 mmol is usual in diabetic ketoacidosis
- [ ] E if hypokalaemic and with a metabolic acidosis the latter should be corrected as quickly as possible

114. Concerning the anion gap

- [ ] A in its estimation serum potassium is discounted
- [ ] B an elevated value indicates a metabolic acidosis
- [ ] C paraldehyde administration causes an increased level
- [ ] D in severe diarrhoea the gap is often normal
- [ ] E carbenicillin may cause an increase in the gap

115. In water homeostasis

☐ A   total body water is equal in both sexes
☐ B   the normal obligate urine output is 1.0 l/day
☐ C   colloid osmotic pressure is 30–40 mm Hg
☐ D   antidiuretic hormone levels are undetectable at a plasma osmolarity greater than 295 mOsmol/kg
☐ E   thirst is normally felt when 2% of the body weight has been lost as water

116. Diabetes mellitus

☐ A   may occur in association with a glucagonoma
☐ B   may occur in association with a somatostatinoma
☐ C   may occur in association with diabetes insipidus
☐ D   may be caused by growth hormone deficiency
☐ E   may be caused by Addison's disease

117. If an elderly patient has hypothermia

☐ A   thrombocythaemia is frequently seen
☐ B   atrial fibrillation is often present
☐ C   plasma viscosity is usually raised
☐ D   the relaxation time of the tendon reflexes is selectively prolonged
☐ E   arterial PCO_2 is often low

In each paper, 2 or 3 questions are on renal medicine topics. Of these, 1 is likely to be about clinical science. These tend to be wide-ranging rather than on any favourite topic. Your revision should cover:

- Glomerular filtration rate (factors affecting)
- Urine discolouration (immediate and on standing)
- Water excretion and concentration
- Nocturia/polyuria
- Complement consumption
- Changes in pregnancy
- Glomerulonephritis

118. Functions of the proximal tubule system include

- ☐ A urinary concentration
- ☐ B pH adjustment
- ☐ C glucose reabsorption
- ☐ D urate reabsorption and secretion
- ☐ E amino acid reabsorption

119. Renal artery stenosis

- ☐ A will usually be due to fibromuscular hyperplasia in a 30-year-old woman
- ☐ B may be treated by percutaneous transluminal angioplasty
- ☐ C is often accompanied by an abdominal bruit
- ☐ D is suggested if there is a disparity in renal size of 1.5 cm or more
- ☐ E will show a delayed nephrogram on intravenous pyelography on the unaffected side

120. Membranous nephropathy

- ☐ A is characterised pathologically by diffuse thickening of the glomerular basement membrane in the absence of a significant increase in glomerular cells
- ☐ B is more frequently recognised in males
- ☐ C may be associated with penicillamine therapy
- ☐ D often presents with macroscopic haematuria
- ☐ E is an HLA associated condition

121. Minimal change nephropathy

- [ ] A   is sometimes known as Alport's syndrome
- [ ] B   usually progresses to renal failure
- [ ] C   is most common in young males
- [ ] D   usually responds promptly to corticosteroid therapy
- [ ] E   produces unselective proteinuria

122. In cystinuria

- [ ] A   there is failure of tubular resorption of cystine
- [ ] B   there may be associated arachnodactyly
- [ ] C   stone formation is aggravated by the presence of an alkaline urine
- [ ] D   penicillamine therapy may be indicated
- [ ] E   the renal stones are always densely opaque

123. During pregnancy

- [ ] A   there is dilatation of the upper urinary tract
- [ ] B   asymptomatic bacteriuria predisposes to acute pyelonephritis
- [ ] C   the endogenous creatinine clearance rate falls during the first trimester
- [ ] D   plasma bicarbonate levels fall
- [ ] E   there is a tendency to retain potassium despite normal plasma potassium levels

124. In the normal adult human (70 kg) each kidney

- [ ] A   weighs approximately 300 g
- [ ] B   has a total nephron population of around 1 million
- [ ] C   receives about 10% of the resting cardiac output
- [ ] D   produces a glomerular filtrate of up to 9 litres/day
- [ ] E   is the major site of 1α-hydroxylation of 25 hydroxycholecalciferol

125. In acute renal failure

☐ A anuria is unusual
☐ B kidney size is reduced
☐ C urinary sodium concentration may be diagnostically helpful
☐ D immediate dialysis is mandatory
☐ E a urine to plasma osmolality ratio greater than 1.5 suggests a pre-renal element

126. In chronic renal failure

☐ A oral magnesium hydroxide is widely used to prevent hyperphosphataemia
☐ B contrast media may further impair renal function
☐ C nocturia is a recognised presenting feature
☐ D progressive renal impairment may be slowed by the use of low protein diets
☐ E gout is a frequent accompaniment of the associated hyperuricaemia

127. Disordered mineral metabolism of chronic renal failure may be manifest by

☐ A pseudoclubbing
☐ B subperiosteal bone resorption
☐ C rugger-jersey spine
☐ D vascular calcification
☐ E Looser's zones

128. In adult polycystic kidney disease

☐ A inheritance is autosomal dominant
☐ B there is an association with berry aneurysms on the circle of Willis
☐ C almost all patients develop end stage renal failure in the fourth decade
☐ D there is an increased incidence of renal tumours
☐ E the genetic mutation is located on the short arm of chromosome 16

129. Urinary tract infection

- ☐ A   may complicate medullary sponge kidney
- ☐ B   can often be treated with a single oral dose of appropriate antibiotic
- ☐ C   may be suggested by a sterile pyuria
- ☐ D   is usually due to *Streptococcus faecalis*
- ☐ E   is not associated with any defect in urinary concentrating ability

130. Renal transplantation

- ☐ A   is contraindicated in SLE
- ☐ B   is associated with an increased incidence of lymphoma
- ☐ C   may be complicated by *Pneumocystis carinii* infection
- ☐ D   is frequently performed across the ABO blood group
- ☐ E   between identical twins has a 90% 1 year graft survival expectation

131. Obstructive uropathy

- ☐ A   may occur with methysergide treatment for migraine
- ☐ B   can result in polyuria
- ☐ C   is associated with tuberculosis
- ☐ D   may be a complication of *Neisseria* infection
- ☐ E   invariably causes an irreversible decline in renal function

132. Discolouration of urine may be due to

- ☐ A   consumption of beetroot
- ☐ B   treatment with isoniazid
- ☐ C   phenylketonuria
- ☐ D   rhabdomyolysis
- ☐ E   acute intravascular haemolysis

133. In type IV renal tubular acidosis, there is

- ☐ A   normal handling of K^+ and H^+
- ☐ B   improvement with fludrocortisone
- ☐ C   association with increased glomerular filtration rate (GFR)
- ☐ D   association with aminoaciduria
- ☐ E   increased bicarbonate in the urine

GASTROENTEROLOGY

There will usually be 4 questions about gastroenterology, including hepatology, biliary and pancreatic disease. One, possibly 2, of these will test your understanding of clinical science. Key topics include:

- Control of acid secretion (and manipulation by drugs)
- Pancreatic function and dysfuntion
- Absorption and malabsorption
- Bilirubin metabolism (jaundice)
- Mechanisms leading to diarrhoea
- Gastrointestinal hormones
- Oesophageal investigations

134. Crohn's disease in elderly people

- [ ] A   is increasing in incidence
- [ ] B   is more common in the distal colon than in younger patients
- [ ] C   can be easily distinguished from diverticular disease when the sigmoid is involved
- [ ] D   has a better prognosis than in younger patients
- [ ] E   is uncommon in the terminal ileum

135. Colonic pseudo-obstruction

- [ ] A   only occurs in elderly people
- [ ] B   can be precipitated by electrolyte imbalance
- [ ] C   produces symptoms identical to colonic obstruction
- [ ] D   can be confirmed by barium enema
- [ ] E   is best treated by surgery

136. Drugs which can induce gastrointestinal ulceration include

- [ ] A   ibuprofen
- [ ] B   doxycycline
- [ ] C   tripotassium dicitratobismuthate (TDB)
- [ ] D   ascorbic acid
- [ ] E   ampicillin

137. Causes of acute ulcerative proctitis include

- [ ] A gonococcus
- [ ] B lymphogranuloma venereum
- [ ] C ischaemia
- [ ] D herpes simplex
- [ ] E *Entamoeba histolytica*

138. In the investigation of malabsorption

- [ ] A a barium examination of the small bowel is mandatory
- [ ] B endoscopic biopsy of the duodenum is adequate to exclude coeliac disease
- [ ] C microscopy of jejunal juice is helpful
- [ ] D chronic pancreatitis is an unlikely diagnosis if there is no radiographic evidence of pancreatic calcification
- [ ] E barium enema examination is a useful procedure to examine the terminal ileum

139. Diarrhoea in a patient with acquired immune deficiency syndrome (AIDS)

- [ ] A may be due to infective proctitis in the anoreceptive homosexual
- [ ] B may be due to *Cryptosporidium*
- [ ] C may require colonoscopy to establish the diagnosis
- [ ] D the faeces should be treated with great caution as they are heavily laden with human immunodeficiency virus (HIV)
- [ ] E may be secondary to small bowel parasites

140. The following are true:

- [ ] A *Campylobacter* species cause acute self-limiting enterocolitis
- [ ] B *Campylobacter* species may cause acute colitis resembling ulcerative colitis
- [ ] C *Campylobacter* species are endemic among domestic animals
- [ ] D *Helicobacter pylori* in the stomach is associated with the presence of erosive gastritis
- [ ] E *Helicobacter pylori* can only be eradicated from the stomach by oral erythromycin

141. Percutaneous liver biopsy

- [ ] A can be performed safely as a day-case procedure
- [ ] B is contraindicated in the presence of ascites
- [ ] C haemorrhage is the commonest complication
- [ ] D biliary peritonitis occurs only in the presence of bile duct obstruction
- [ ] E antibiotic prophylaxis is necessary in patients with cardiac valvular disease

142. Fatty infiltration of the liver

- [ ] A also affects the spleen
- [ ] B may be patchy rather than uniform
- [ ] C can be reliably diagnosed using ultrasound and computer tomography making biopsy unnecessary
- [ ] D can occur in patients on total parenteral nutrition
- [ ] E in alcoholics is usually totally reversible with abstinence

143. Bile acid diarrhoea

- [ ] A occurs in terminal ileal disease of any cause
- [ ] B can be treated with oral cholestyramine
- [ ] C may cause gallstone formation in the gall bladder
- [ ] D may be caused by surgery
- [ ] E may be associated with blood in the stools

144. Hepatic adenoma

- [ ] A is the most commonly occurring benign liver tumour
- [ ] B is associated with oral contraceptive use
- [ ] C is a premalignant lesion
- [ ] D has a characteristic appearance on ultrasound examination
- [ ] E may be multiple

145. In the treatment of duodenal ulcer

☐ A a single daily dose of H_2 receptor antagonists is as effective as multiple doses

☐ B patients with ulcers resistant to H_2 receptor antagonists should have the dose increased

☐ C the recurrence rate is influenced by the choice of initial drugs for treatment

☐ D patients who fail to respond to treatment with H_2 antagonists after two months should be tested for *Helicobacter pylori*

☐ E recurrence after successful treatment may be entirely asymptomatic

146. In acute upper gastrointestinal haemorrhage

☐ A oesophageal mucosal tears as a cause are rare

☐ B patients who are hypovolaemic and hypotensive on admission are more likely to rebleed

☐ C a risk of recurrent bleeding can be predicted by endoscopic findings

☐ D early surgery is to be avoided in elderly people

☐ E a duodenal ulcer is more likely to rebleed than other lesions

147. Oesophageal varices

☐ A acute bleeding can be controlled using somatostatin infusion

☐ B do not occur after surgical oesophageal transection

☐ C the risk of bleeding is proportional to the size of the varix

☐ D are less likely to bleed than gastric varices

☐ E risk of recurrent haemorrhage can be reduced by endoscopic sclerotherapy

148. Ultrasound examination of the biliary system

☐ A is as accurate as oral cholecystography in demonstrating gall bladder calculi

☐ B will demonstrate the cause of bile duct obstruction in over 50% of cases

☐ C can diagnose biliary carcinoma

☐ D yields approximately 5% false-negative results in differentiating bile duct obstruction from non-obstructive jaundice

☐ E is performed in the fasting patient

149. In halothane hepatotoxicity

- ☐ A death can occur from liver failure after a single exposure
- ☐ B liver damage occurs due to hypoxia during anaesthesia
- ☐ C it can be easily differentiated from viral hepatitis
- ☐ D liver transplant is appropriate therapy for severe fulminant hepatic failure
- ☐ E mortality is greater after repeated exposure

150. In a patient undergoing enteral feeding

- ☐ A diarrhoea can be avoided by giving the feed in boluses
- ☐ B diluted initiating regimes to prevent diarrhoea are usually unnecessary
- ☐ C the smaller bore tubes have a lower incidence of oesophageal ulceration
- ☐ D in a non-catabolic patient the calorie requirement is 30–35 cal/kg/day
- ☐ E hyperglycaemia may be induced

In the exam, there will be 2–3 questions on haematology, with most being disease linked. For clinical science, you should have reasonable knowledge of:

- Clotting – pathways, abnormalities, anticoagulants (see pharmacology)
- Iron, B_{12} and folate metabolism
- Outline of stem cell – differentiated cell pathway
- Haemolysis
- Methaemoglobinaemia
- ABO system and blood transfusion
- Use of blood products (fresh frozen plasma)
- Mechanisms for macrocytosis

151. In disseminated intravascular coagulation (DIC)

- ☐ A   thrombocytopenia is rare
- ☐ B   factors V and VIII are among the first to be consumed
- ☐ C   fibrin degradation products (FDPs) are almost always elevated
- ☐ D   the FDPs have a coagulant effect
- ☐ E   heparin therapy is the treatment of choice

152. The following are recognised complications of paroxysmal nocturnal haemoglobinuria (PNH):

- ☐ A   pancytopenia
- ☐ B   acute leukaemia
- ☐ C   renal failure
- ☐ D   iron deficiency anaemia
- ☐ E   Budd–Chiari syndrome

153. The following conditions may be associated with secondary erythrocytosis:

- ☐ A   hydronephrosis
- ☐ B   carboxyhaemoglobinaemia
- ☐ C   hepatoma
- ☐ D   leishmaniasis
- ☐ E   uterine leiomyoma

154. A peripheral blood basophilia may be associated with the following:

- [ ] A chronic myeloid leukaemia
- [ ] B urticaria pigmentosa
- [ ] C ulcerative colitis
- [ ] D myelofibrosis
- [ ] E secondary polycythaemia

155. The following features are well associated with Henoch–Schönlein disease:

- [ ] A thrombocytopenia
- [ ] B severe types of glomerulonephritis
- [ ] C a positive Hess test
- [ ] D cirrhosis
- [ ] E abdominal pain

156. In chronic lymphatic leukaemia (CLL)

- [ ] A immunoglobulin levels are usually elevated
- [ ] B thrombocytopenia indicates a more advanced stage of the disease
- [ ] C associated haemolytic anaemia is usually due to cold-type antibodies
- [ ] D chest infections are a common cause of morbidity and mortality
- [ ] E cellular immunity is well preserved

157. In haemophilia A (classical haemophilia)

- [ ] A the bleeding tendency is usually more severe than in haemophilia B (Christmas disease)
- [ ] B the prothrombin time is a good screening test in diagnosis
- [ ] C factor IX may be of therapeutic use in specific clinical situations
- [ ] D cerebral haemorrhage is the commonest cause of death
- [ ] E most cases of chronic hepatitis are due to hepatitis C virus

158. In von Willebrand's disease (VWD)

- ☐ A the bleeding time is usually normal
- ☐ B the vascular endothelium shows abnormalities under the light micro-scope
- ☐ C haemarthrosis is commoner than in haemophilia
- ☐ D transfusion of haemophiliac plasma to a patient with VWD can result in a rise in the factor VIII level
- ☐ E consanguineous marriage can result in more clinically severe cases

159. Macrocytic non-megaloblastic anaemia may be found in

- ☐ A liver disease
- ☐ B hypothyroidism
- ☐ C aplastic anaemia
- ☐ D strict vegetarians
- ☐ E hypopituitarism

160. Monoclonal gammopathy (paraprotein) is a recognised association with the following:

- ☐ A acute lymphoblastic leukaemia (ALL)
- ☐ B chronic myeloid leukaemia
- ☐ C chronic lymphatic leukaemia (CLL)
- ☐ D cold haemagglutinin disease (CHAD)
- ☐ E acute myeloid leukaemia (AML)

161. Glucose-6-phosphate dehydrogenase (G6PD) deficiency

- ☐ A occurs more commonly in men than women
- ☐ B may be associated with increased haemolysis after taking oxidant medication
- ☐ C may be associated with neonatal jaundice
- ☐ D produces a characteristic spherocytic haemolytic anaemia
- ☐ E is more common in Sephardic Jews

162. In sickle cell anaemia

☐   A   folate supplements may prevent aplastic crises
☐   B   haptoglobins are raised
☐   C   serum iron is low
☐   D   aseptic femoral head necrosis may occur
☐   E   priapism is a recognised complication

INFECTIOUS AND TROPICAL DISEASES

The number of infectious disease questions in the general medicine module has fallen since the development of the paediatric exam and the movement of questions on childhood infectious diseases to the new module. However, there will still be 3–4 questions on infections. Within these, the role of clinical science is not as clear as in some of the other subjects, but it is definitely there. You need to consider:

- Mechanism of action of antimicrobials, and development of resistance to them
- Disordered immunity and infection (could be considered within immunology)
- Vaccination mechanisms
- Routes of transmission (faecal–oral, vectors)
- Interpretation and alteration of tuberculosis immunity

163. The following statements are true of infective diarrhoeal illness:

- ☐ A   rotavirus is a common cause in bacterial culture negative adult cases
- ☐ B   *Clostridium difficile* toxin associated illness responds to vancomycin
- ☐ C   the use of erythromycin in *Campylobacter* infections prolongs the carriage rate
- ☐ D   the presence of sigmoidoscopical/histological changes of colitis virtually excludes salmonellosis
- ☐ E   parental vaccination is a very effective prophylaxis against cholera

164. In the toxic shock syndrome

- ☐ A   significant hypotension invariably occurs
- ☐ B   prevalence has decreased to very low levels following the withdrawal of hyperabsorbent tampons
- ☐ C   an elevated creatinine phosphokinase is found in about 40% of cases
- ☐ D   symptoms can recur
- ☐ E   treatment should be with parenteral benzylpenicillin

165. In typhoid fever

- [ ] A rose spots are pathognomonic
- [ ] B biochemical hepatitis is common
- [ ] C amoxicillin is as effective a therapy as chloramphenicol
- [ ] D intestinal perforation should be managed non-surgically
- [ ] E focal neurological signs can occur

166. The following are true of the Epstein–Barr virus:

- [ ] A it is responsible for most cases of infectious mononucleosis occurring after blood transfusion
- [ ] B it produces a dormant episomal state in B-lymphocytes
- [ ] C it is associated with the Duncan syndrome
- [ ] D corticosteroids may be useful in the treatment of severe glandular fever
- [ ] E ampicillin associated rashes occur in 90% of cases

167. In meningococcal meningitis

- [ ] A sporadic cases are most often due to Group A organisms
- [ ] B hypo-adrenalism consistently occurs if meningococcaemia is present
- [ ] C intravenous benzylpenicillin should be withheld pending definitive lumbar puncture diagnosis
- [ ] D endotoxin mediated haemorrhagic oedema is a common mode of death
- [ ] E rifampicin chemoprophylaxis should be administered to household contacts

168. In acquired immune deficiency syndrome (AIDS)

- [ ] A patients presenting with Kaposi's sarcoma have a better prognosis than those with *Pneumocystis carinii* pneumonia
- [ ] B a rash occurs in about a third of patients given co-trimoxazole
- [ ] C thrombocytopenia is a recognised complication
- [ ] D there is a high prevalence in the heterosexual population in some African countries
- [ ] E *Toxoplasma gondii* can produce mass CNS lesions

169. In Lassa fever

- ☐ A the diagnosis should be considered in a patient returning from central Africa with a fever of at least 4 weeks' duration following departure
- ☐ B *Mastomys natalensis* is the rodent vector
- ☐ C thrombocytopenia is usually found
- ☐ D there is a hospital case fatality rate of 15–25%
- ☐ E person to person spread occurs

170. In Legionnaires' disease

- ☐ A gastrointestinal symptoms are uniquely characteristic
- ☐ B cigarette smoking and heavy alcohol consumption are risk factors
- ☐ C rifampicin alone is as effective as erythromycin in treatment
- ☐ D strict barrier nursing is essential
- ☐ E cerebellar ataxia occurs

171. In tuberculous meningitis

- ☐ A in the UK it is the commonest form of non-respiratory TB
- ☐ B measurement of CSF glucose is a useful guide in diagnosis
- ☐ C intrathecal antibiotics should be given
- ☐ D the initial CSF is usually positive on ZN staining
- ☐ E approximately a quarter of survivors have residual neurological disease

172. In acute osteomyelitis

- ☐ A the commonest organism is *Streptococcus pyogenes*
- ☐ B incidence is highest in elderly people
- ☐ C spread is usually haematogenous
- ☐ D radiological changes are diagnostic within 24 hours of onset
- ☐ E blood cultures are useful

173. In ^{111}Indium leucocyte scanning

☐   A   maximal sensitivity of detection of sepsis is not reached for 24 hours
☐   B   the cells are taken up by bowel and kidney
☐   C   false positives may occur within haematomas
☐   D   areas of involvement in inflammatory bowel disease may show
☐   E   acute pancreatitis may be localised

174. When considering the use of hepatitis B vaccine

☐   A   the carriage rate of hepatitis B virus is about 1 in 1000 of the population in Britain
☐   B   the presence of the antibody to hepatitis 'e' antigen indicates a highly infectious state
☐   C   the vaccine is produced against the 'e' antigen
☐   D   the vaccine is prepared by recombinant DNA technique
☐   E   given alone it carries a high protection rate to babies born to carrier mothers

175. The following are true regarding human prion disease:

☐   A   the abnormal human prion protein is produced from the same gene as the normal prion protein
☐   B   abnormal prion protein may be inactivated by UV light
☐   C   human prion disease may be transmitted by inoculation of the host
☐   D   abnormal prion protein induces a significant local inflammatory response
☐   E   the protein contains high levels of nucleopeptides

176. HIV infection results in

☐   A   impaired interleukin 2 production
☐   B   inhibition of polyclonal B cell activation
☐   D   impaired presentation of antigen by major histocompatibility complex
☐   D   increased β_2 microglobulins
☐   E   infection of macrophages

The exam will contain 1–2 questions on rheumatological conditions, with overlap into metabolic (bone) conditions and immunology. Common basic science topics include:

- Normal joint physiology – synovium and fluid
- Immunology of rheumatoid disease
- Predisposition to sero-negative arthropathies (HLA etc.)
- Uric acid metabolism
- Mechanisms leading to osteoporosis
- Disturbed immune function in SLE
- Antiphospholipid antibody syndrome

177. The following statements are correct:

☐ A   cranial arteritis is uncommon under the age of 55
☐ B   renal failure and hypertension are the commonest cause of death in polyarteritis nodosa
☐ C   in rheumatoid vasculitis the kidney is rarely involved clinically
☐ D   characteristic histological features of polyarteritis nodosa are small vessel granulomata
☐ E   Waldenstrom's macroglobulinaemia is associated with a necrotising vasculitis

178. Osteoporosis

☐ A   is due to impaired mineralisation of osteoid
☐ B   can be secondary to immobilisation
☐ C   may present with thoracic nerve root compression
☐ D   can result from regular calcitonin administration
☐ E   is associated with reduced hydroxyproline excretion

179. Synovial fluid

☐ A   is produced by the joint capsule
☐ B   is reduced in viscosity in inflammatory arthritis
☐ C   contains abundant lymphocytes in rheumatoid arthritis
☐ D   may contain positively birefringent crystals in gout
☐ E   if heavily bloodstained is most probably due to malignancy

180. In rheumatoid arthritis

☐ A   Rose Waaler and latex agglutination tests measure IgG rheumatoid factor
☐ B   nodules are rare in seronegative patients
☐ C   the presence of splenomegaly and leucopenia is usually due to the development of amyloidosis
☐ D   keratoconjunctivitis sicca is a common complication
☐ E   the platelet count is often elevated in active disease

181. In polymyositis

☐ A   most adult patients will have underlying neoplasia
☐ B   ocular muscle weakness is rare
☐ C   polyphasic motor unit action potentials are elicited on electromyography
☐ D   the onset is usually rapid
☐ E   muscle biopsy is always positive

182. In scleroderma

☐ A   Raynaud's phenomenon is a late feature
☐ B   the disease is characteristically preceded by the occurrence of morphoea
☐ C   the CREST syndrome usually occurs in association with rapidly progressive systemic sclerosis
☐ D   anticentromere antibodies are highly specific
☐ E   reduced carbon monoxide diffusion capacity is often present early in the disease

183. The following statements are correct:

☐ A   gonococcal arthritis often affects more than one joint
☐ B   an arthritis similar to early rheumatoid arthritis may occur with rubella infections
☐ C   in tuberculous arthritis the organisms are often seen in synovial fluid cultures
☐ D   Reiter's syndrome may be triggered by *Shigella* dysentery
☐ E   circinate balanitis is a feature of Reiter's syndrome

184. The following statements are correct:

☐ A   the HLA B27 status frequently changes to positive during the onset of ankylosing spondylitis
☐ B   patients with Reiter's disease are more likely to be HLA B27 positive than the normal population
☐ C   HLA DR4 status is associated with an increased relative risk of rheumatoid arthritis
☐ D   HLA antigens are present on the cell membranes of both T and B lymphocytes
☐ E   a positive HLA B27 status is required to diagnose ankylosing spondylitis

185. Typical joint involvement includes

☐ A   the distal interphalangeal (DIP) joints in rheumatoid arthritis
☐ B   the first carpo-metacarpal (CMC) joint in osteoarthritis
☐ C   the wrist joints in pseudogout
☐ D   the sacroiliac joints in systemic lupus erythematosus
☐ E   the thoracolumbar spine in diffuse idiopathic skeletal hyperostosis (Forrestier's disease)

186. The following are true:

☐ A gout is characterised by the presence of crystals of monosodium urate monohydrate
☐ B uric acid is a product of haemoglobin metabolism
☐ C high dose aspirin is uricosuric
☐ D pseudogout is caused by sodium diphosphonate crystals
☐ E commencement of allopurinol therapy can precipitate an acute attack of gout

187. The following statements are correct:

☐ A membranous glomerulonephritis is a recognised complication of D-penicillamine treatment
☐ B D-penicillamine is a chelating agent of divalent cations
☐ C treatment with gold can cause an amyloid nephropathy in patients with longstanding rheumatoid arthritis
☐ D cataracts occur more commonly in iatrogenic Cushing's syndrome than in Cushing's syndrome from other causes
☐ E ocular complications of hydroxychloroquine therapy include corneal deposits

188. In systemic lupus erythematosus

☐ A anti double standard DNA antibodies are highly specific
☐ B drug-induced lupus occurs more readily in fast acetylators
☐ C nephrotic syndrome is the commonest manifestation of renal involvement
☐ D complement levels are often raised
☐ E lymphopenia is more frequent than neutropenia

Immunology has increased in the examination, which mirriors the growth in its importance in medical practice. There will usually be 2 questions in the paper; of these, 1 will normally be on 'bread and butter' immunology such as 'the following are true of IgA'.

Important topics include
- Immunoglobulins – IgA, IgM, IgG, IgE
- Cell mediated immunity
- Important cytokines (e.g. tumour necrosis factor α)
- Interferons α, β (relevant in hepatology, neurology)
- Disturbed immunity in HIV infection (question in most exams about AIDS)
- Hypersensitivity reactions
- Tissue receptor antibodies
- T lymphocytes
- Leukotrienes (e.g. asthma)
- Transplant immunology
- Immune complexes
- Role of complement (e.g. nephrology, rheumatology)

189. The following cross the placenta:

☐ A IgG
☐ B IgM
☐ C unconjugated bilirubin
☐ D heparin
☐ E thyroid stimulating immunoglobulin (TSI)

190. Selective IgA deficiency

☐ A may be associated with transfusion reactions
☐ B if symptomatic, may be associated with IgG3 subclass deficiency
☐ C has an approximate UK prevalence of 1 in 10,000
☐ D usually has preserved normal salivary IgA antibodies
☐ E is associated with coeliac disease

191. Anti-neutrophil cytoplasmic antibodies (ANCA)

- [ ] A suggest Wegener's granulomatosis
- [ ] B often disappear after treatment of vasculitis
- [ ] C have specificity for neutrophil polysaccharides
- [ ] D are found in polyarteritis nodosa
- [ ] E result in bacterial infections due to neutropenia

192. The lupus anticoagulant

- [ ] A usually presents with haemorrhage
- [ ] B may be responsible for recurrent fetal loss
- [ ] C is an antiphospholipid antibody
- [ ] D affects the lipid-soluble clotting factors
- [ ] E is associated with thrombocytopenia

193. The Ro (SS-A) extractable nuclear antigen antibody

- [ ] A is found in neonatal lupus syndrome
- [ ] B may be found in the absence of antinuclear antibody
- [ ] C is diagnostic of systemic sclerosis
- [ ] D is associated with livedo reticularis of the skin
- [ ] E may be associated with congenital heart block

194. IgG subclass 2

- [ ] A may be absent in selective IgA deficiency
- [ ] B is the first IgG subclass to develop after birth
- [ ] C may be low or absent in recurrent childhood infections
- [ ] D is particularly associated with allergic responses
- [ ] E fixes complement via the alternate pathway

195. In AIDS

☐   A   the ratio of helper to suppressor cells is the best marker of progression
☐   B   combination treatment with reverse transcriptase inhibitors is not superior to single therapy
☐   C   the virus most commonly encountered in the UK is HIV2
☐   D   only lymphocytes are infected by HIV
☐   E   HIV-seropositive haemophiliacs are not an infection risk for their spouses

The fear that statistics generates is entirely out of proportion to its representation in the exam. At most it will only comprise 1 question or 1.7% of the marks available. The reason why people fail is not because of poor statistical knowledge but weaknesses in cardiology, neurology, pharmacology and so on, which comprise a much greater proportion of the questions. Even so, with a little preparation it is possible to gain a few marks in the statistics question. Important topics include:

- Definitions of mean, median and mode
- Standard deviations, errors
- When to apply parametric and non-parametric tests
- Correlation coefficients (r)
- Normal distributions (including t distribution) and skewed distributions
- Tests of significance (probability)

You might also want to consider some more recent developments:

- Confidence intervals and limits
- Risk – relative and absolute, number needed to treat (evidence based medicine)
- Clinical trials.

196. When considering the results of a clinical trial involving two treatments

☐ A if $p = 0.50$ the results must have occurred by chance
☐ B the confidence limits of the result are inversely proportional to the number in the trial
☐ C the chance of making a type II error is dependent on the number in the trial
☐ D if the difference between the treatments is large the confidence limits are of less importance
☐ E if $p = 0.10$ then the result could occur by chance in one in ten trials

197. In a trial of two anti-epileptic drugs following head injury 18 out of 27 patients treated by drug A were fit free one month after injury compared with 5 out of 17 patients treated with drug B. If the significance of these results is tested by the chi-squared test

- ☐ A   the figures should first be converted to percentages
- ☐ B   the test is non-parametric
- ☐ C   there is one degree of freedom
- ☐ D   a value of chi-squared of 4.3 would imply that the result would have been obtained by chance in 43 out of 100 trials
- ☐ E   the results would be invalidated if most of the cases treated with drug A had developed the arrhythmia immediately after the head injury compared with those treated with drug B

198. A study finds that tallness in a child as compared with its siblings has values of r = 0.6, $p < 0.001$

- ☐ A   r is the correlation coefficient of probability
- ☐ B   if $p < 0.001$ it means that the result is highly significant
- ☐ C   if $p < 0.001$ it means that too few measurements have been made
- ☐ D   if r < 1 then a negative correlation exists
- ☐ E   there is a linear relationship

199. The standard deviation of a group of observations

- ☐ A   is the square of the variance of the group
- ☐ B   is a measure of the scatter of the observations around the mean
- ☐ C   is a valid statistical parameter only if the observations have a normal distribution
- ☐ D   is numerically higher than the standard error of the mean
- ☐ E   may be used as a basis for the calculation of chi-squared

200. The following are correct:

☐ A $p = 0.01$ is a lower degree of statistical significance than $p = 0.05$
☐ B the prevalence of ischaemic heart disease varies in different areas of the UK
☐ C in a frequency distribution the mode is the most frequently observed value
☐ D the median is the point on a scale of values which exactly divides the number of values into upper and lower halves
☐ E the incidence of a disorder means the number suffering from that disorder at any one time

201. In a normal (Gaussian) distribution

☐ A the mode is the most frequent observation
☐ B the median divides the distribution exactly into two halves
☐ C the mean, median and the mode are numerically the same
☐ D the distribution is numerically the same as a Poisson distribution
☐ E all the people in the sample are normal

DERMATOLOGY

There will probably be 1 question on dermatology in the paper. Mostly, these will be disease related, but some may test knowledge of disordered immunity. You should consider:

- Skin manifestations of systemic disease
- Immunology and the skin
- Vasculitides – mechanisms

202. Granuloma annulare

☐ A is more common on the trunk
☐ B is painful
☐ C is associated with diabetes
☐ D may persist for many years
☐ E has the histological appearance of collagen necrobiosis

203. The following are true of pyoderma gangrenosum:

☐ A it may respond to high dose corticosteroids
☐ B it is associated with paraproteinaemias
☐ C it may predate the onset of inflammatory bowel disease
☐ D there is no association with Crohn's disease
☐ E development is linked to local trauma

204. In susceptible individuals urticaria may be precipitated by

☐ A vibration
☐ B a virus infection
☐ C salicylates
☐ D benzoic acid
☐ E tartrazine

205. In a patient with lichen planus

- ☐ A lesions may be observed at the site of trauma
- ☐ B oral lesions are only seen in the minority of cases
- ☐ C nail damage may occur
- ☐ D chronic oral lichen planus is a pre-malignant condition
- ☐ E B-lymphocyte infiltration is usually seen on biopsy

206. The following are true of rashes seen in syphilis:

- ☐ A chancres are painful ulcers seen in primary syphilis which typically heal spontaneously within 3–6 weeks.
- ☐ B vesicular rashes are often seen late in secondary syphilis
- ☐ C the rash of secondary syphilis begins on the trunk and spreads to the periphery, especially to the palms and soles
- ☐ D the hair follicles are unaffected by infection
- ☐ E spirochaetes can be readily visualised by dark ground microscopy of material from skin gummas

MOLECULAR AND GENETIC MEDICINE

Since the division into general medicine and paediatric modules in 1993, most exams have included questions relating to molecular and genetic medicine. Many candidates find these difficult, but, as the College has pointed out, the knowledge tested is regularly covered by reviews and editorials in the prime medical journals (*Lancet, British Medical Journal* and the *New England Journal of Medicine*). If you have time, you may want to look through some back copies of these. You should remember, however, that the exam is set a year in advance and topical items will not appear.

Some things that you might want to consider include:

- Definition of terms (e.g. introns, exons etc.)
- Polymerase chain reactions
- Genetic predisposition to disease
- Linkages
- Oncogenes
- Mitochondrial DNA function
- Genetic anticipation

207. The polymerase chain reaction

☐ A   is used to copy proteins
☐ B   can be used to study RNA
☐ C   can determine whether a gene is making a specific protein
☐ D   can be used to identify amino acid substitutions
☐ E   can detect very small quantities of nucleic acid

208. In the mechanisms responsible for asthma

☐ A   a single gene defect predisposes individuals
☐ B   polymorphisms of the β_2 adrenoreceptor are linked to disease severity
☐ C   a characteristic is down-regulation of a subclass of T helper cells
☐ D   there is a decreased expression of interleukin 4, 5 and 9
☐ E   major intra-cellular second messengers are phospholipase C and adenylate cyclase

209. The following are correct:

- ☐ A the main role of tumour necrosis factor α is in catabolism
- ☐ B adhesion molecules govern the emigration of leucocytes into the tissues
- ☐ C apoptosis is accidental cell death
- ☐ D the extracellular matrix is composed of lipids and proteins
- ☐ E a chemokine is a cytokine which repels leucocytes

210. The following are true:

- ☐ A an allele is an alternative form of a gene which occupies a different position on a chromosome
- ☐ B the e4 allele is related to the development of Alzheimer's disease
- ☐ C linkage analysis is used to determine the position of genes responsible for particular diseases
- ☐ D transcription factors promote gene expression
- ☐ E knock-out mice have increased expression of the gene of interest

211. In p53 genetic abnormalities

- ☐ A the gene is located on chromosome 17
- ☐ B the normal gene prevents exit from the S phase of the cell cycle
- ☐ C both somatic and germline mutations occur
- ☐ D screening for mutation is available
- ☐ E somatic mutations are associated with colonic carcinoma

ANSWERS AND TOPIC SUMMARIES

CARDIOLOGY

1.   Anatomy of the coronary arteries   **Answers: AE**

Normally the right coronary artery (RCA) supplies the right atrium, part of the left atrium, right ventricle and sinoatrial node (may be supplied by the circumflex artery). The posterior descending artery is a terminal branch of the RCA supplying the posterior third of the IV septum, and the AV node. It may anastomose with the left anterior descending (LAD) artery around the apex of the left ventricle.

The left main stem coronary artery bifurcates to provide the LAD and circumflex coronary arteries. In approximately 30% of people an intermediate vessel arises at the site of division. The LAD runs in the anterior interventricular groove and supplies the anterior two-thirds of the IV septum and the anterior surface of the LV including the apex.

The circumflex branch of the left coronary artery lies in the posterior atrioventricular groove to supply the posterior cardiac wall and obtuse margin.

2.   Phaeochromocytoma   **Answers: ABD**

No single (one-off) test can exclude the diagnosis.

24-hour urinary excretion of VMA is used as a screening test, but false negatives may occur if the tumour is intermittently excreting adrenaline or noradrenaline. However, three normal 24-hour collections virtually exclude the diagnosis. False positives may be found unless certain items are excluded from the diet e.g. bananas, pineapple and vanilla ice cream.

Plasma adrenaline and noradrenaline can be measured; the levels vary with sympathetic activity, but with repeated measurements the results can be very reliable – particularly plasma noradrenaline.

In the pentolinium suppression test, sympathetic ganglia are blocked and the plasma levels of adrenaline and noradrenaline fall except in the presence of autonomous production, as in a phaeochromocytoma. However, the response is erratic and may be excessive, so they are rarely used.

Once a biochemical diagnosis is made, the tumour needs to be localised. A CT scan of the abdomen (adrenals, sympathetic chain and bladder) is usually helpful as the tumours are often very large. A MIBG scan can be performed which relies on the uptake of amine precursors.

Urinary 5HIAA is a derivative of 5 hydroxytryptamine and is raised in carcinoid syndrome not in phaeochromocytoma.

3.   Chronic constrictive pericarditis   **Answer: B**

In chronic constrictive pericarditis the heart size is usually normal.

Atrial fibrillation is common and occurs in up to 50% of cases, and the ECG may show other changes including low voltage QRS complexes and generalised T wave inversion.

A pericardial friction rub is not usually heard but a loud diastolic 'knock' similar in timing to a 3rd heart sound but of higher pitch, is characteristic.

Elevation of the jugular venous pressure always occurs and it rises further with inspiration (Kussmaul's sign). The arterial pressure and pulse pressure are low because of the impaired ventricular filling, pulsus paradoxus is uncommon and rarely exceeds 15 mm Hg.

Echocardiography may show a thickened pericardium. The ventricles fill rapidly in early diastole, but the appearances are similar to constrictive cardiomyopathy.

4.   Heart transplant   **Answers: ABCE**

One of the first markers of organ rejection is a systemic pyrexia. Signs of heart failure are usually late.

Chest pain is not a symptom of rejection.

Frequent checks are made on cardiac size on chest radiograph since an increase is a feature of rejection as are changes in the ECG including conduction abnormalities and reduction in QRS voltages.

Serial percutaneous endomyocardial biopsies may be helpful.

5.   Cardiac anatomy   **Answers: AD**

There is normally 60–100 ml of pericardial fluid. Several litres may collect without compromising cardiac function provided the accumulation is slow. If the pericardial volume is suddenly expanded, atrial and ventricular filling are impaired and tamponade results.

The coronary circulation drains into the coronary sinus which normally empties into the right atrium.

The normal cardiac weight is less than 400 g and is increased in ventricular hypertrophy. Echocardiography is very useful in estimating left ventricular mass (e.g. in hypertension). The left/right ventricular mass ratio should be 2.3–3.3:1.

The transverse cardiac diameter changes during systole and diastole by up to 1 cm but diameters greater than 50% of the largest transthoracic diameter are abnormal.

The oesophagus lies in close proximity to the posterior cardiac chambers (left atrium and ventricle).

6. **Mitral stenosis**   **Answers: All false**

In mitral stenosis there is obstruction to the forward flow of blood between the left atrium (LA) and left ventricle (LV). This results in an elevation of the LA pressure which is transmitted through the pulmonary capillary bed causing an elevation in the pulmonary wedge pressure (PWP). Thus the PWP is an indirect measurement of LA pressure.

The increase in LA pressure causes dilatation of the atrium which can produce widening or splaying of the carina. This is sometimes seen on a penetrated PA chest radiograph.

Dilatation of the LA causes increased atrial ectopic activity with the eventual development of atrial fibrillation in most cases, but by no means all. The combination of atrial fibrillation, obstructed LA outflow and LA dilatation causes turbulence of blood in the LA with intra-atrial thrombosis and systemic embolism which is virtually abolished by oral anticoagulants.

A chest infection can cause an increase in pulmonary pressure which if it is sufficiently elevated by the coexistent mitral stenosis will precipitate pulmonary oedema. This is not left ventricular failure since the LV is small in pure mitral stenosis.

The surgical treatment of mitral stenosis depends more on the pathology of the valve than on the age of the patient. If the valve is thin and pliable without significant calcification or incompetence, a valvotomy is usually acceptable and desirable. However, in most elderly patients the valve is thick, distorted and calcified, requiring valve replacement.

7. The normal electrocardiograph   **Answers: CDE**

The PR interval should be greater than 0.11 and less than 0.20 seconds. A long PR interval implies atrioventricular node dysfunction and, in isolation, is referred to as first degree heart block. A short PR interval may represent a pre-excitation syndrome e.g. Lown–Ganong–Levine syndrome or when associated with a QRS duration of greater than 0.11 seconds and slurring of the initial 0.03-0.05 seconds of the QRS complex, Wolff–Parkinson–White syndrome.

The normal mean frontal QRS axis is –30 degrees to +90 degrees. An axis more negative than –30 degrees is termed left axis deviation (LAD) and an axis more positive than +90 degrees is termed right axis deviation (RAD). Causes of LAD include left anterior hemiblock, inferior myocardial infarction, ventricular pre-excitation, hyperkalaemia, tricuspid atresia, ostium primum atrial septal defect and artificial cardiac pacing. Causes of RAD include left posterior hemiblock and right ventricular hypertrophy.

R wave amplitude may vary in the limb leads. It should not exceed 13 mm; values higher than this reflect left ventricular hypertrophy (LVH). Other diagnostic features of LVH include R wave in aVF greater than 20 mm, R in V4–6 greater than 27 mm, S in V2 or V3 greater than 30 mm or the combined largest S wave in V1–3 and largest R wave in V4–6 of greater than 40 mm.

Right bundle branch block (RBBB) may be a normal finding. When it develops suddenly it may be a feature of acute right heart strain as in pulmonary embolus or a feature of right ventricular hypertrophy. It may be rate dependent, occurring with fast heart rates because the right bundle has a longer refractory period than the left.

A Q wave in lead III is a normal finding. Pathological Q waves exceed 0.04 seconds in duration and have a depth greater than one quarter of the height of the ensuing R wave.

8. Thyroid heart disease   **Answers: ABCDE**

In hyperthyroidism, there is increased drive which causes predictable cardiac changes e.g. sinus tachycardia, high cardiac output with low peripheral resistance resulting in a collapsing pulse. Systolic hypertension is common and diastolic hypertension can occur in up to 30% of patients.

In the normal heart, these changes in sympathetic drive do not usually cause overt problems. However, in elderly people and in patients with pre-existing heart disease, hyperthyroidism may precipitate heart failure and cardiac arrhythmias (especially atrial fibrillation) and exacerbate angina.

Beta-adrenoreceptor blocking drugs are very effective in countering the increased sympathetic drive due to hyperthyroidism and can be used with caution in patients with overt heart failure.

Hypothyroidism causes the opposite effects; bradycardia, low cardiac output, hypotension and fluid retention including pleural and pericardial effusions. Correction of the biochemical abnormality with a small dose of thyroxine will cause the effusions to disappear.

Several ECG changes can occur with hypothyroidism including prolongation of the QT interval, low P and T wave and QRS amplitude and atrioventricular and intraventricular conduction disturbances e.g. right bundle branch block.

9. **Congenital heart disease**   **Answers: BCD**

There are two types of ASD, ostium primum and ostium secundum. In ostium primum defects, the defect is close to the atrioventricular valves in the lower part of the interatrial septum and is part of an endocardial cushion defect. There is often an associated abnormality of the atrioventricular valves and sometimes a VSD (complete AV canal defect). Ostium primum defects are associated with other congenital abnormalities e.g. Down's syndrome, asplenia and polysplenia. The ECG may show left axis deviation and right ventricular hypertrophy with prolongation of the PR interval.

Ostium secundum ASD are far more common than primum ASD. Patients are usually asymptomatic in early life and most are diagnosed by health screening. The physical findings include a prominent right ventricular heave, split second heart sound, pulmonary systolic flow murmur and tricuspid diastolic flow murmur. The ECG usually shows right axis deviation, right ventricular hypertrophy and rSR or rsR pattern in the right precordial leads with a normal QRS duration. A prolonged PR interval may occur.

Ventricular septal defect is the commonest congenital heart defect occurring in about 30% of all cases. ASD and patent ductus arteriosus (PDA) account for about 10% each.

All the inherited connective tissue disorders can have cardiac manifestations. Aortic incompetence occurs with Marfan's syndrome, Ehlers–Danlos syndrome and osteogenesis imperfecta. Peripheral and coronary vascular disease can occur with Ehlers–Danlos syndrome and pseudoxanthoma elasticum.

The recurrence risk in siblings of affected children with congenital heart disease is small, about 5% for VSD and less for all the others.

10. Circulatory changes in pregnancy   Answers: ADE

Cardiac output rises in the first trimester of pregnancy by 30–50%. This change is accompanied by increases in stroke volume and ejection fraction. There is a rise in resting heart rate by about 10 beats/minute which is relatively constant up to term.

Blood volume rises rapidly in early pregnancy until about mid-pregnancy and continues to increase slowly until term. The overall rise in blood volume is of the order of 40–50%. This increment is higher in twin pregnancies and in multigravidae than in primigravidae.

Systemic arterial blood pressure falls in pregnancy with a proportionately greater fall in diastolic pressure producing a wider pulse pressure. The blood pressure rises towards non-pregnant levels just before delivery.

Pulmonary arterial pressure remains normal throughout pregnancy which, in view of the increased cardiac output, implies a fall in pulmonary vascular resistance.

11. Fallot's tetralogy   Answers: ABC

The two essential features of Fallot's tetralogy are a large ventricular septal defect (usually sited in the membranous part of the septum) and stenosis of the pulmonary valve or infundibulum. These result in resistance to blood flow through the pulmonary valve and consequently a right to left shunt.

Typically the infant is pink at birth with cyanosis developing over the next few weeks or months and being most apparent with the exertion of crying or feeding.

Vasodilatation, such as in a hot environment, will increase the shunt. Squatting traps venous blood in the legs and compresses the femoral arteries. This causes a raised aortic pressure that will reduce the shunt.

12. Jugular venous pressure   Answers: AB

There are 3 waves (a, c, v) that reflect (in order) atrial contraction, tricuspid valve closure and venous filling of the superior vena cava (SVC) and jugular veins during the period when the tricuspid valve is closed.

There are two descents. The x descent is due to the fall in atrial pressure during ventricular systole because of downward movement of the base of the heart. The y descent is the collapse of the column of venous blood from the SVC into the ventricle when the tricuspid valve opens.

The fourth heart sound is also a consequence of atrial contraction and thus coincides with the 'a' wave while the third heart sound is a result of early diastolic filling of the ventricle and coincides with the 'y' descent.

In the absence of right ventricular dysfunction, the hepatojugular reflex is transient and rarely exceeds 1 cm.

13. Change in posture   Answers: ABE

Squatting increases peripheral resistance and consequently the aortic pressure. The gradient between the aortic root and the left ventricle is increased in diastole with a subsequent increase in flow into the ventricle across a regurgitant aortic valve.

The rise in aortic pressure results in early aortic valve closure with an increase in end systolic volume. In turn, this leads to an increase in ventricular pressure and volume during the early phase of diastole. The 4th heart sound is intensified by; firstly, a rise in ventricular volume (decreased ventricular compliance); and secondly, by an elevation in ventricular pressure during early diastole which then causes an increase in atrial emptying that must occur during atrial systole (late diastole).

Squatting diminishes the gradients across the ventricular septal defect in Eisenmenger syndrome and across the outflow obstruction in hypertrophic obstructive cardionyopathy.

The increase in end diastolic volume results in an increase in the time required for the ventricular volume during systole to fall to the level at which mitral valve prolapse occurs.

14. Broad complex tachycardia   **Answers: BE**

The following favour ventricular tachycardia
  i)   A-V dissociation
  ii) S1 varying in intensity
  iii) Left axis deviation
  iv) Duration of QRS > 140 ms
  v)   Fusion beats
  vi) Capture beats
  vii) Concordance

15. Valsalva manoeuvre   **Answer: A**

The haemodynamic changes resulting from a Valsalva manoeuvre are different in its various phases.

Analysis of the changes in intensity and character of a murmur during phase 2 is the most useful. There is a decrease in venous return, right and left ventricular volumes, stroke volumes, mean arterial pressure, and pulse pressure, with a reflex increase in heart rate.

The decreased flow across the valves results in a diminution of the murmurs of stenosis or regurgitation of aortic, pulmonary, mitral and tricuspid valves. Conversely, the murmur of hypertrophic obstructive cardiomyopathy increases as the left ventricular outflow size decreases with decreased venous return.

The decreased left ventricular volume results in the systolic click of mitral valve prolapse occurring earlier in systole such that occasionally it may coincide with S1.

16. Reversed splitting of the second heart sound   **Answers: BCE**

Reversed splitting occurs when the aortic component of S2 is delayed so that A2 and P2 occur together during inspiration and P2 precedes A2 during expiration.

This may be caused by a conduction disturbance (left bundle branch block, Wolff–Parkinson–White syndrome with a right sided accessory pathway, right ventricular (RV) pacing, ventricular ectopic beats of RV origin) or mechanical causes (aortic stenosis, PDA, aortic regurgitation).

Causes of wide splitting of S2 include right bundle branch block, left ventricular pacing, Wolff–Parkinson–White syndrome with a left sided accessory pathway, pulmonary stenosis and pulmonary hypertension.

Fixed splitting occurs with atrial septal defects.

17. Infective endocarditis   Answer: E

Microorganisms responsible for infective endocarditis:

	Native valve	Prosthetic valve	Drug abuse
Strep viridans	+++	++	Very rare
Staph aureus	+	++	+++
Staph epidermidis	+	++	+
Enterococcus	+	+	+
Other Strep.*	++	+	++
Gram -ve bacilli	+	+	++
Culture -ve	+	+	+

* Includes S. milleri, S. mutans, S. mitis and S. mitior.

Polymicrobial infections are rare.

The risk of endocarditis is higher in the presence of high pressure abnormal flow (i.e. MR >MS, VSD>ASD) and prostheses.

10–15% of patients may have no murmur on initial examination, although most will develop one.

18. Nitric oxide   Answers: BC

Nitric oxide (NO) is a potent vasodilator and works via a pathway which is distinct from that of prostacyclin. It is manufactured by NO synthetase, three forms of which have been identified: endothelial, neuronal and macrophage.

In addition to vasodilatation NO also prevents platelet and white cell aggregation as well as acting as a neurotransmitter and having some immune functions.

The main target for NO is the enzyme guanylate cyclase which is activated by NO with subsequent rises in cGMP levels (not cAMP). The clinical effects of nitrates (e.g. isosorbide mononitrate) are mediated via NO as their active moiety.

19. **Selective alpha-blockade** **Answers: BCE**

All the alpha-blockers in clinical use (terazosin, prazosin, doxazosin) inhibit the post-synaptic alpha1 receptor with resultant relaxation of vascular smooth muscle and vasodilatation. Despite this, a reflex tachycardia is uncommon.

Alpha receptors are found in the bladder neck and prostatic capsule and the use of alpha-blockers is associated with increased urinary flow rates.

Studies have shown a decrease in total cholesterol, VLDL, LDL and triglycerides with an increase in HDL in long-term use.

There may be a reduction in left ventricular mass in patients with hypertension and LV hypertrophy.

An increase in plasma glucose is not observed in alpha-blockade, unlike beta-blockade.

20. **Physiological murmurs** **Answers: ABD**

Physiological murmurs are usually short systolic murmurs, but venous hum is a continuous murmur.

Venous hum is best heard with the patient upright or sitting and is abolished by supine position and jugular pressure.

Vibratory and physiological pulmonary murmurs are heard best with the patient supine and increase in intensity on exercise or fever. Diastolic murmurs are usually pathological.

CLINICAL PHARMACOLOGY

21. Antiemetics   Answer D

The induction of vomiting is controlled by the emetic centre which is situated close to the floor of the 4th ventricle. It is the final common pathway for stimuli arising from several sites including: the chemoreceptor trigger zone (CTZ) on the surface of the 4th ventricle, vestibular apparatus, meninges, cerebral cortex, and gastrointestinal tract via vagus and sympathetic afferents. There are high concentrations of dopamine receptors in the emetic centre and the CTZ with associated cholinergic and histamine (H_1) receptors.

Metoclopramide, the phenothiazines, butyrophenones, and domperidone reduce vomiting predominantly by antagonism at dopamine receptors. Domperidone crosses the blood–brain barrier poorly and has a peripheral mode of action. Metoclopramide also has some peripheral action through increased gastro-oesophageal sphincter tone and stomach emptying due to increased cholinergic activity. It is used in high dose (2 mg/kg) in oncology and can produce oculogyric crises (acute dopamine blockage).

Other drugs used to control vomiting include the cannabinoids and benzodiazepines, particularly after cytotoxic chemotherapy. Anticholinergics and antihistamines are particularly effective in vomiting induced by motion sickness.

The $5HT_3$ antagonists have changed the outlook for patients undergoing chemotherapy with the most emetic regimes (e.g. those containing platinum).

22. Lithium therapy   Answers: DE

Lithium therapy is used prophylactically in patients with unipolar and bipolar affective disorders. If used in the treatment of mania it requires 7–10 days to take effect. It has also been used in schizophrenia.

Lithium is slowly excreted via the kidney with an initial half-life of approximately 18–20 hours. The therapeutic range is 0.4–0.8 mmol/l. Some clinicians accept higher levels than this, but above 1.5 mmol/l the incidence of toxic effects rises (increased thirst, nausea, diarrhoea, and neurological signs such as slurred speech, coarse tremor, ataxia, confusion and fits). At levels above 2.5 mmol/l marked toxicity is usually apparent and is an indication for dialysis.

Transitory symptoms, particularly at the initiation of therapy, include metallic taste, nausea, altered bowel habit, weight gain and thirst. More persistent harmless abnormalities include leucocytosis, ECG and EEG changes.

Potential drug interactions involve diuretics (Na depletion), NSAIDs, phenothiazines, carbamazepine and phenytoin. All of these can increase toxicity particularly the neurological abnormalities.

Breast feeding is contraindicated as lithium readily crosses into the milk. The drug is also associated with congenital malformations including cardiac abnormalities and neonatal goitre.

23. Prescribing in renal failure Answer: B

When you are answering questions on prescribing in liver or renal failure, you need to know the proportion of drug excreted by any one route.

Doxycycline is the only tetracycline which is safe in renal failure; all the others cause a rise in urea production and a negative nitrogen balance with an increase in sodium excretion.

Insulin is inactivated by the kidney. In renal failure, insulin requirements may fall dramatically. The sulphonylureas can induce prolonged hypoglycaemia. The use of metformin (biguanides) can precipitate lactic acidosis.

The efficacy of any drug in treating a urinary infection is dependent on the amount appearing in the urine. Both nitrofurantoin and nalidixic acid are poorly excreted and should be avoided. Apart from cephaloridine the cephalosporins and the penicillins (not carbenicillin because of its high sodium content) are effective in a reduced dose.

Potassium sparing diuretics should be avoided particularly in diabetics. The loop diuretics (frusemide, ethacrynic acid and bumetanide) are effective but the risk of toxicity (VIII nerve) is increased. The thiazides are ineffective at a low glomerular filtration rate.

24. Antiplatelet drugs Answers: ADE

The theoretical use of antiplatelet drugs is based on the balance between prostacyclin (a natural anticoagulant) released by the vascular endothelium and thromboxane produced by platelets in response to vascular damage.

Both substances are generated by the cyclo-oxygenase rather than the lipoxygenase pathway.

Aspirin in doses between 75 and 325 mg reduces the risk of stroke (or other vascular events) by approximately 30%. The higher the dose (including 325 mg) the greater the risk of gastrointestinal bleeding. At a dose of 75 mg, the production of thromboxane is abolished, until the enzyme is regenerated through the release of new platelets. The vascular endothelium can renew cyclo-oxygenase once the level of aspirin falls.

The non-steroidal anti-inflammatory drugs block cyclo-oxygenase, but have little effect on lipoxygenase in normal therapeutic dosage. NSAIDs can stimulate bronchoconstriction by diverting precursors down the lipoxygenase pathway. The effect of aspirin in provoking asthma is much greater and is an idiosyncratic response.

25. Anticonvulsant drugs   Answers: AE

Apart from carbamazepine and phenytoin, all other anticonvulsants are well absorbed orally. When given intramuscularly absorption is again poor for these two drugs as well as diazepam. The intravenous route is preferred in the unconscious patient for diazepam (or rectally) and phenytoin. This ensures a predictable level for a given iv dose.

Anticonvulsants are heavily protein bound and are susceptible to drug interactions. Phenytoin, phenobarbitone and carbamazepine are also potent enzyme inducers. Carbamazepine induces its own metabolism so increased dosage is required with time.

Lamotrigine works by reducing glutamate activity (an excitatory amino-acid neurotransmitter). Vigabatrin and gabapentin work by increasing the levels of GABA – an inhibitor neurotransmitter.

Apart from phenytoin (exponential) and possibly ethosuximide in high dose the relationship of the dose to plasma level is linear. The anticonvulsant effect of sodium valproate is not simply related to the amount in the plasma, i.e. the biological half-life is greater than the plasma half-life.

26. Treatment of schizophrenia   Answers: ACE

The antipsychotic effect of the neuroleptics is proportional to their antidopaminergic action. They also possess to a variable extent anticholinergic, antiadrenergic and antihistamine (H_1) actions. The side-effects of the different agents can be predicted by knowledge of these. Haloperidol has a relatively reduced anticholinergic effect, thus its antagonism at dopamine receptors in the basal ganglia is unopposed and extrapyramidal symptoms are increased.

As with galactorrhoea (dopamine is the prolactin release inhibiting hormone), the dopamine antagonism often leads to weight gain.

Many studies have shown that although patients do relapse on treatment (less than 50%), the rate is significantly lower than for patients taking a placebo, and is dependent on the duration of illness prior to treatment and the features (relationship to life events, affective overlay etc) of the psychosis.

Clozapine differs from conventional neuroleptics and is used in resistant schizophrenic illness. It has potent alpha-adrenoceptor blocking, anticholinergic, antiserotoninergic and antihistaminergic action.

27. Malignant hyperpyrexia   Answers: BCDE

Malignant hyperpyrexia is an autosomal dominant inherited condition in which there is a defect in the calcium transport function of the sarcoplasmic reticulum of muscle. When exposed to halothane or suxamethonium, an acute rise in intracellular calcium takes place which leads to rigidity, muscle necrosis, hyperpyrexia and severe metabolic acidosis. Progression to acute renal failure subsequently occurs with a very high mortality.

The syndrome may also be precipitated by tricyclic antidepressants, enflurane or monoamine oxidase inhibitors. A similar picture is seen with high dose neuroleptics (malignant neuroleptic syndrome).

Diazepam, thiopentone, fentanyl citrate and nitrous oxide appear safe as are tubocurarine and althesin.

The diagnosis is made *in vitro* by exposure of muscle to halothane or suxamethonium.

Treatment consists of the discontinuation of the offending agent, correction of acidosis and hyperkalaemia, cooling, and general circulatory support. Procaine, procainamide and dantrolene sodium have been used as specific treatments. Dantrolene blocks the influx of calcium ions from the sarcoplasmic reticulum in response to depolarisation.

28. Anti-tuberculous drugs and the liver   Answers: CDE

Both rifampicin and isoniazid cause transient rises in hepatic aminotransferases. However, a true hepatitis may develop. The risk of hepatotoxicity with isoniazid is increased in those patients who are fast acetylators (cf neuropathy – slow acetylators).

The main side-effect of pyrazinamide is hepatotoxicity and regular checks (2–4 weeks) of liver function (AST, ALT) need to be done. The other main problem is increasing uric acid levels and precipitating gout. It is contraindicated in breast feeding.

Streptomycin (renal and VIII nerve toxicity) and ethambutol (optic neuritis) are excreted by the kidney.

29. Drugs and the eye   Answers: AB

The effects of drugs on the eye should be divided into actions on the optic nerve, retina, cornea and conjunctiva. Chloroquine (bull's eye macula) in a dose greater than 250 mg/day for 1 year has a high incidence of toxic retinopathy. Thioridazine (but not other phenothiazines) in a very high dose of 600–800 mg/day can also induce a retinopathy.

Ethambutol, and rarely streptomycin or isoniazid, can produce an optic neuritis.

The corticosteroids (a dose of ≥ 10 mg/day for 1 year or more) produce a high incidence of posterior subcapsular cataracts. The phenothiazines, as in the cornea, can produce pigment granules in the lens but these rarely interfere with vision.

Chloroquine and amiodarone cause corneal microdeposits but these do not interfere with vision.

Remember there may be severe keratitis in drug-induced Stevens–Johnson syndrome.

30. Drug-induced interstitial nephritis   Answers: ABCDE

Acute interstitial nephritis appears to be immunologically mediated and is not usually dose related. Fever, rashes, arthralgia, eosinophilia etc often accompany the immune nephritis. Renal biopsy is often characteristic and ultrasound may show enlarged kidneys. Treatment with corticosteroids may be beneficial.

Apart from the drugs listed in the question others implicated include sulphonamides and thiouracils (similar chemical structure to thiazides).

When considering drug effects on the kidney, group them into those causing acute tubular necrosis, vasculitis, drug-induced lupus and glomerulonephritis.

The following have been implicated in the nephrotic syndrome, but only account for 2% of cases: penicillamine (immune mediated), captopril (high dose), gold salts, phenindione, probenecid and tolbutamide.

No lists given in the sections on the side-effects of drugs on any particular system are complete or exhaustive!

31. Pharmacokinetics in elderly people   Answers: All false

The pharmacokinetics of drugs in elderly people can be considered in terms of absorption, protein binding and volume of distribution, target organ responsiveness, and drug excretion.

Apart from an increasing incidence of achlorhydria, the absorption of drugs changes very little with age. Similarly, serum albumin, being the major determinant of protein binding, falls only slightly, if at all, in fit old people. Both fat stores and lean body mass decline with age, the latter to a greater extent especially in the very old.

Target organ responsiveness changes with age, the brain being more susceptible to the effects of hypnotics or sedatives. In contrast the cardio-vascular response to drugs (e.g. propranolol) declines.

Glomerular filtration rate starts to decline after the age of 30 years; approximately 1 ml/min/yr is lost, the fall being linear with time. The ability of the liver to metabolise drugs does not change but hepatic blood flow and drug extraction reduces with increasing years. Thus drugs with a large first pass effect (i.e. propranolol, nitrates, or verapamil) are affected, a larger proportion reaching the systemic circulation.

32. Pharmacokinetics in pregnancy   Answers: DE

In pregnancy, the increase in plasma volume and total body water alters the volume of distribution. The average weight gain of 3–4 kg of adipose tissue also increases the reservoir for fat-soluble compounds (e.g. diazepam, anaesthetics). Albumin is decreased by up to 10 g/l in the first half of pregnancy. Hence, protein binding/unit volume falls and a new equilibrium has to be established between free and bound drug with an overall reduction in plasma levels. Hepatic clearance increases in pregnancy which affects drugs such as phenytoin. Renal plasma flow and glomerular filtration rate are almost doubled by term. Drugs that are excreted unchanged in the urine have an increased rate of clearance, for example the plasma levels of ampicillin are lower in pregnancy.

Drugs are transferred to the fetus by passive diffusion, the rate being determined by molecular size and lipid solubility. Peak levels are usually reached within 0.5–2.0 hours. Metabolism does occur in the fetal liver but excretion is mainly through the mother. The placenta contributes very little to drug metabolism.

33. The benzodiazepines   Answers: ABCD

Apart from the oral benzodiazepines available for general use, clobazam, diazepam and clanazepam are also available for use in epilepsy. They are readily grouped into: long acting (diazepam, chlordiazepoxide and nitrazepam), short acting (temazepam, lorazepam and oxazepam), and very short acting (triazolam and midazolam, (only available intravenously).

The half-life of diazepam as a single dose is much shorter because of redistribution compared with regular therapy. In chronic dosage, its half-life ranges from 20–90 hours and increases considerably with age. The metabolite desmethyl diazepam is also active with a very long half-life.

Those drugs excreted as glucuronides (lorazepam and oxazepam) are affected by renal impairment, but not by poor liver function. Diazepam and the other benzodiazepines are generally contraindicated in cirrhosis.

The benzodiazepine receptor is widely distributed. The ageing brain is more sensitive to benzodiazepines.

Flumazanil is a specific benzodiazepine antagonist. It has a short half-life and so the sedation (and respiratory depression) caused by long acting benzodiazepine agonists may reappear as the effect of flumazanil wears off. It can cause seizures, particularly in epileptic patients.

34. Digoxin overdose   Answers: CDE

The pharmacology and pharmacokinetics of digoxin and related cardiac glycosides is a common examination topic. In overdose the potassium level rises (Na-K ATPase pump depression) which protects the myocardium to some extent. Hypokalaemia predisposes to digoxin toxicity.

The symptoms of digoxin toxicity can be grouped into: (i) gastrointestinal – nausea, anorexia, vomiting, and abdominal pain; (ii) CNS – xanthopsia (yellow-green vision), blurring of vision, and confusion especially in elderly people; (iii) cardiac – any arrythmia may occur. The most serious are ventricular, but the commonest is simply a sinus bradycardia with first degree block.

First line treatment is to correct any hypokalaemia (but not hyperkalaemia) and monitor the cardiac rhythm. In patients with serious arrhythmias (e.g. ventricular or haemodynamic instability), Fab fragments of antibodies to digoxin are the treatment of choice. These have a low incidence of immune reactions, lacking the Fac portion, and often produce a dramatic response by mopping up the free drug.

The loading dose of digoxin is related to body mass and associated volume of distribution. Maintenance dose is then dependent on the glomerular filtration rate (GFR). The 0.0625 mg tablet is usually too small for fit elderly people. Serum levels are only a guide to dosage (less than 2.5 µg/l) and if toxicity is suspected the drug should be withdrawn. Digitoxin is metabolised in the liver and except at GFR less than 10 ml/min it may be used in renal impairment but it has a very long half-life.

The definite indication for digoxin is in the control of the ventricular rate in atrial fibrillation. It can be used in atrial flutter but will increase the rate of atrial repolarisation.

Digoxin is contraindicated in supraventricular arrhythmias associated with accessory pathways and also in hypertrophic obstructive cardionyopathy.

35. Salicylate poisoning   Answers: CD

Symptoms of salicylate poisoning become apparent when the blood level exceeds 300 mg/l (tinnitus, sweating) and above 500 mg/l active treatment is indicated. The management is: mild poisoning (<500 mg/l – fluid correction and monitoring electrolytes; moderate (<500 mg/l plus acidosis or <750 mg/l alone) – alkaline diuresis or oral activated charcoal; severe (<750 mg/l plus renal impairment or <900 mg/l alone) – charcoal haemoperfusion or haemodialysis. Forced alkaline diuresis carries a high mortality and very good salicylate excretion can be achieved by fluid repletion and urine alkalinisation.

The symptoms and signs of severe poisoning include:

*   nausea, vomiting and epigastric discomfort
*   hyperpyrexia and sweating
*   irritability, tremor and deafness
*   pulmonary oedem;
*   hypokalaemia and either hyper- or hyponatraemia
*   respiratory alkalosis (except in children) followed by metabolic acidosis and eventually respiratory acidosis;
*   hyper- or hypoglycaemia and hypoprothrombinaemia (may be corrected in part by vitamin K_1).

Consciousness is often retained until the final stages of poisoning.

Owing to gastric stasis and the tablets forming a slowly dissolving bolus, gastric lavage is indicated as aspirin levels can rise for up to 24 hours after the overdose.

36. Angiotensin-converting enzyme (ACE) inhibitors   Answers: AE

ACE inhibitors are now a frequent exam topic. They competitively inhibit the conversion of the decapeptide angiotensin I to the octapeptide angiotensin II, causing a fall in aldosterone production. Enalapril is a pro-drug and the onset of any hypotension after the initial dose is delayed for 2–3 hours. Half-life is captopril<enalapril<lisinopril. The initial haemodynamic effect of ACE inhibitors is mediated through inhibition of membrane-bound endothelial ACE and ACE in the renal cortex and myocardium as well as plasma ACE. Additionally, ACE inhibitors may also increase vagal activity resulting in hypotension and bradycardia.

ACE inhibitors also block the degradation of bradykinin and it is likely that many of their beneficial effects are mediated by this pathway. Aspirin has an inhibitory effect on bradykinin synthesis and to a minor degree inhibits some of the effects of ACE inhibition.

Owing to the fall in aldosterone, the serum potassium rises fairly consistently and the concurrent use of potassium supplements or potassium-sparing diuretics is contraindicated.

In patients with renal artery stenosis, renal perfusion is often solely dependent on the renin–angiotensin system and inhibition can precipitate thrombosis within the artery as the perfusion falls.

Apart from hypotension, side-effects after captopril are usually mild such as gastrointestinal, rashes, disturbance of taste etc. At high dose, neutropenia and the nephrotic syndrome have been described. In low dose, mild proteinuria is sometimes found.

ACE inhabitors improve survival in patients with heart failure and also following myocardial infarction in patients with a low ejection fraction (<35%).

37. Antidotes   Answers: ABDE

There are five groups of antidotes.

- Those forming an inert complex with the poison.
  Arsenic, mercury, gold: dimercaprol
  Lead: penicillamine, calcium sodium edetate
  Iron: desferrioxamine
  Thallium: Prussian blue
  Cholinesterase inhibitors: pralidoxime

- Those increasing the rate of metabolism to a less toxic compound.
  Cyanide: thiosulphate
  Paracetamol: methionine or N-acetylcysteine

- Those reducing the rate of metabolism.
  Methanol: ethanol

- Those competing for essential receptor sites.
  Carbon monoxide: oxygen
  Opiates: naloxone
  (N.B. effects of partial agonists such as buprenorphine or pentazocine)

- Those blocking essential receptors.
  Anticholinesterases: atropine.

38. Drugs and folate metabolism   Answers: ABCD

Folic acid is a vitamin only for mammals. (The definition of a vitamin is an essential compound supplied by the diet which cannot be synthesised, so is vitamin D a vitamin?) Bacteria produce folic acid from para-aminobenzoate by dihydroptoeroate synthetase. Subsequently dihydrofolate is metabolised by dihydrofolate reductase to tetrahydrofolate and eventually folinic acid is formed.

The sulphonamides compete as an analogue of p-aminobenzoate and hence inhibit the formation of folic acid in bacteria.

Pyrimethamine in protozoa and trimethoprim in bacteria have an extremely high affinity for dihydrofolate reductase compared with the mammalian enzyme. Methotrexate inhibits the mammalian enzyme, hence its use in oncology. Folinic acid can be given to bypass these enzymatic stages before normal cells are irreparably damaged.

39. Vaughan-Williams classification   Answer: E

The classification is:

Type 1   drugs all act chiefly by blocking the fast sodium channels responsible for depolarization.

Type 1a (disopyramide, procainamide, quinidine) also prolong repolarization.

Type 1b (lignocaine, mexiletine, tocainide, phenytoin) also accelerate repolarization.

Type 1c (flecainide, propafenone) do not affect repolarization.

Type 2   drugs are beta-blockers.

Type 3   drugs act by blocking potassium channels responsible for repolarization (e.g. amiodarone, bretylium, sotalol).

Type 4   drugs are calcium antagonists (i.e. verapamil, diltiazem).

Drugs that prolong the action potential (1a and 3) predispose to Torsade de Pointes. Amiodarone has effects in all four classes. Sotalol has type 2 and type 3 effects. Digoxin and adenosine do not fall into any class.

40. Adenosine   Answers: CDE

Adenosine is a naturally occurring purine nucleoside. It has effects on all cardiac tissues, but its chief clinical value is in its inhibitory effect on atrioventricular nodal conduction. This is mediated by A_1 receptors, which are coupled to G-proteins. These, in turn, cause hyperpolarization by increasing opening of potassium channels.

Adenosine also suppresses sinus node automatically and reduces atrial refractoriness and accessory pathway refractoriness, which underlies its potential to precipitate atrial tachyarrhythmias.

The half-life of adenosine is around 2 seconds. The cellular degradation of adenosine is inhibited by disopyramide with a subsequent prolongation of half-life. Theophylline is an antagonist of A_1 receptors.

41. Gentamicin therapy   Answers: BCE

The dosing interval should be set from the glomerular filtration rate or the blood urea level. If treatment is prolonged beyond 2 weeks then toxicity may develop despite appropriate therapeutic levels.

The recommended peak levels are 4–10 μg/ml. Often, the clinical aim is for slightly higher peaks of 6–10 μg/ml.

If the trough level is high and the peak is acceptable, then the dosing interval should be increased.

Several drugs may precipitate the toxic effects of gentamicin. These include frusemide – causing ototoxicity. First generation cephalosporins such as cephaloridine, and cisplatin and amphotericin B may produce nephrotoxicity.

42. Non-steroidal anti-inflammatory drugs (NSAIDs) Answers: All false

The prime action is to block the cylco-oxygenase pathway producing various inflammatory mediators (prostaglandins). One potential consequence is an overactivity of the lypo-oxygenase pathway with increase in leukotrienes which may produce asthma. In aspirin-induced asthma, there is a hypersensitivity reaction over and above this mechanism.

Another consequence of cyclo-oxygenase blockade is a reduction of intra-renal generation of prostaglandins. This can have deleterious effects on intra-renal vascular control causing a deterioration in renal function and hyperkalaemia.

The most important problem is an increased risk of the complications of peptic ulcers, particularly in older people. The use of rectal preparations, pro-drugs, or enteric-coated drugs does *not* protect against gastric damage.

Ibuprofen appears the safest NSAID with diclofenac and naproxen being relatively safe despite their stronger anti-inflammatory action. The mechanism of gastric mucosal damage is again linked to alteration in prostaglandin production. Misoprostol, which is a prostaglandin analogue, helps prevent damage to the mucosal surface.

There are other problems with NSAIDs, for example fluid retention and resistance to treatment for heart failure or hypertension (particularly with indomethacin).

43. Tamoxifen in breast carcinoma   Answers: AE

Tamoxifen acts by competing with oestradiol for a cytoplasmic receptor. In practice approximately 50% of patients with advanced carcinoma who are receptor positive will respond and 15% of receptor negative patients will also derive benefit.

Tamoxifen has an active metabolite, desmethyl tamoxifen, and both have a half-life of approximately 2 weeks. Steady state is therefore not reached for at least 6 weeks after starting therapy.

Response is probably as frequent in pre- as in post-menopausal women and is strongly predictive of future benefit from other endocrine treatment (e.g. oophorectomy).

The drug is well tolerated. Tumour growth may increase in the first few weeks because of agonist activity and hypercalcaemia may appear. The median time to response is approximately 6 months. Symptoms of oestrogen deficiency may become apparent. Fluid retention occasionally occurs.

44. Medical factors in the use of oral contraceptives   Answer: D

There is no evidence that progesterone alone increases blood pressure. Even in low dose, the combined oestrogen and progesterone contraceptive pill increases arterial pressure. Established or developing hypertension is therefore a contraindication to a combined pill.

Oestrogens increase the risk of arterial or venous thrombosis in some women. The progesterone only preparation appears safe.

If a woman of over 35 years smokes then the risk of serious cardiovascular events is greatly elevated if she is receiving a combined but not a progesterone only pill.

Certain tumours may be oestrogen sensitive e.g. malignant melanoma, hepatoma, desmoid tumours or carcinoma of the breast.

As with oestrogens, the metabolism of progesterone is increased by the concurrent use of anticonvulsants that are hepatic enzyme inducers.

The combined preparations probably do not enhance the risk of thrombotic crises in sickle cell disease.

Other relative medical contraindications for the use of a combined pill include diabetes with arteriopathy, hepatic disease and previous jaundice/pruritus in pregnancy.

45. Warfarin   Answers: ABC

The BNF states that ampicillin may increase the prothrombin time by a few seconds (broad spectrum antibiotic).

In drug interactions with warfarin, consider two effects.

* Displacement of warfarin from the protein binding site (e.g. sulphonamides, NSAIDs and sulphonylureas). A new steady state is then established. Consequently, the danger is at the start or end of therapy.
* Enzyme inhibition or competition (e.g. cimetidine).

The most common interaction is protein displacement. The most serious is enzyme inhibition.

Enzyme induction can have the opposite effect (e.g. rifampicin, griseofulvin and carbamazepine).

RESPIRATORY MEDICINE

46. Transfer factor   Answers: ADE

Athletes have increased cardiac output and probably an increase in pulmonary capillary blood volume.

The loss of alveolar walls and capillaries reduces the surface area available for carbon monoxide to combine with haemoglobin. In addition there is ventilation/perfusion mismatching causing a reduction in transfer factor.

A right to left shunt causes a reduction in pulmonary capillary blood volume and pulmonary hypertension may cause ventilation – perfusion mismatching. The opposite causes increased transfer factor.

Recent pulmonary haemorrhage with functioning haemoglobin available in alveolar spaces causes an increase in transfer factor because of the increase in uptake of carbon monoxide. In diseases such as pulmonary haemosiderosis (including Goodpasture's syndrome), between attacks of acute pulmonary haemorrhage, the transfer factor is often reduced because of pulmonary fibrosis and the interstitial lung disease.

47. Pulmonary compliance   Answers: ACDE

As compliance is a measure of how easily the lung (and chest wall) may be stretched, any interstitial lung disease or chest wall disease causing increased stiffness (and therefore resistance to stretch) will cause reduction in compliance.

The fibrosis of fibrosing alveolitis and long standing mitral stenosis will cause increased stiffness of the lungs and therefore a reduction in compliance. A similar reduction occurs due to the oedema and hyaline membrane formation of ARDS.

Reduction in overall alveolar tissue (as in emphysema) causes less resistance to stretch and therefore increases compliance.

48. Oxygen–haemoglobin dissociation curve   Answers: ABDE

Remember, the 'RIGHT' thing for haemoglobin to do in muscles is to give up oxygen and moving the haemoglobin–oxygen dissociation curve to the RIGHT causes this to happen. The conditions which would be expected to prevail in working/stressed muscles include:

- a rise in CO_2 due to increased metabolism
- an increase in hydrogen ion concentration (i.e. a fall in pH)
- an increase in temperature.

These things therefore move the haemoglobin–oxygen dissociation curve to the RIGHT. It would also be 'RIGHT' for oxygen to be given up easier in chronic hypoxic states and chronic anaemia, (which causes an increase in red cell 2, 3-diphosphoglycerate.

49. Respiratory physiology   Answers: AC

The main carina normally moves 2–3 cm during inspiration and expiration.

The upper lobe bronchi arise posterolaterally. In the supine position, the effects of gravity preferentially deposit aspirated material into these lobes. In the erect posture, the right main bronchus is more vertical than the left and therefore is more liable to aspiration.

The main resistance to airflow is in the trachea/larynx. Relatively small lesions here cause major airways obstruction. The total cross-sectional area of the respiratory bronchioles is approximately 10 times that of the trachea.

Type I pneumocytes are the low-flat cells forming the blood-gas barrier. Type II pneumocytes secrete and store a surface-acting agent (surfactant) which causes a reduction in surface tension preventing alveolar collapse.

50. Carbon dioxide retention   Answers: BC

Hypoventilation, as in muscular weakness from Guillain–Barré syndrome, causes retention of carbon dioxide.

Patients with chronic bronchitis tend to hypoventilate and retain carbon dioxide relatively early in the disease.

Patients with emphysema, fibrosing alveolitis and pulmonary emboli tend to hyperventilate and the $PaCO_2$ is normal or low. However, in advanced (almost pre-terminal) emphysema and fibrosing alveolitis, and in massive pulmonary embolus, retention of carbon dioxide may occur.

51. Sleep apnoea syndrome   Answers: BD

Sleep apnoea syndrome can be divided into obstructive (commonest) and central. The main symptoms are snoring (in obstructive variety), insomnia, nocturnal choking and/or panic attacks, hypnogogic hallucinations and nightmares. Other problems include morning headache (CO_2 retention), depression, personality change and impotence.

Patients with sleep apnoea syndrome (Pickwickian syndrome) are usually obese.

Chronic nocturnal hypoxia causes pulmonary vascular constriction with resultant pulmonary hypertension and eventually right ventricular failure.

Patients should be treated by withdrawal of any sedatives (including alcohol) that may aggravate hypoventilation, strict dieting to achieve predicted body weight and diuretics etc to treat right ventricular failure. Progesterones have been used as respiratory stimulants.

Nocturnal nasal continuous positive airways pressure (c-PAP) has produced good benefits.

52. Acquired immune deficiency syndrome   Answers: ABDE

Owing to profound immunosuppression, these patients are prone to opportunist infections such as *Pneumocystis*, CMV, *Cryptococcus neoformans* and a number of atypical mycobacteria such as *Mycobacterium avium, M. intracellulare* and *kansasii*.

Patients with AIDS are prone to developing Kaposi's sarcoma which may occur in the lungs as well as in the skin and many other body tissues.

Pulmonary veno-occlusive disease belongs to the rare group of pulmonary hypertensions of unexplained aetiology. Because post-capillary vessels are involved and therefore the capillaries themselves are not protected from the hypertension, these patients develop pulmonary oedema early. There is no association with AIDS.

53. Bronchoalveolar lavage fluid   Answer: C

The finding of asbestos bodies in sputum and alveolar lavage fluid is only a reflection of exposure to asbestos and is *not* diagnostic of asbestosis.

Alveolar lavage fluid in sarcoidosis is characteristically associated with an increase in lymphocytes due to the T lymphocyte alveolitis.

The cell count in bronchoalveolar lavage is expressed as an estimate of total cell count and also as a proportionate differential count. Smokers often have both an absolute increase in cell count and also proportionally more polymorphs and macrophages than non-smokers.

There is some overlap in cell count and differential count between the different types of alveolitis (fibrosing alveolitis, sarcoidosis, extrinsic allergic alveolitis etc) and bronchoalveolar lavage may act better as a guide to disease progress and response to treatment than as a diagnostic tool. The finding of non-caseating granulomata at bronchial or transbronchial biopsy is very suggestive of sarcoidosis. Bronchial mucosal biopsies may be positive when the macroscopic appearance is normal.

54. Carcinoma of the bronchus   Answers: ACD

An FEV$_1$ of less than 2 litres (or 50% of the volume predicted) suggests that a patient undergoing pneumonectomy (as in this case) would be left with inadequate pulmonary reserve.

The left recurrent laryngeal nerve runs an intrathoracic course, hooking under the aortic arch, and is often involved in carcinoma of the bronchus. However, it is quite unusual for the right recurrent laryngeal nerve to be involved since this only descends as far as the subclavian artery. Another cause for a palsy should be sought before declaring the patient inoperable.

A wide fixed carina suggests extensive mediastinal disease and if the tumour is within 1 cm of the carina it will be, in most cases, technically inoperable.

Hypercalcaemia may be caused by multiple bony metastases but with squamous cell carcinoma a more common cause is a hormonal, non-metastatic parathormone-like effect.

55. α$_1$ anti-trypsin deficiency   Answers: DE

The sex incidence is equal. It should be suspected in anyone developing emphysema, in the under 40s and also in non-smokers.

The panlobular emphysema is usually more marked at the bases and the appearances are generally of greater severity with a worse prognosis in smokers.

Since α$_1$ anti-trypsin is an acute phase protein, levels may rise to within the normal range during acute infections, particularly in heterozygous patients. A low level of α$_1$ anti-trypsin level in venous blood should prompt definition of the phenotype. There are said to be 21 different phenotypes, but in everyday practice the normal is MM, homozygote ZZ and heterozygote MZ.

56. Fibrosing alveolitis   Answers: BDE

Cough is a frequent and often troublesome symptom.

Polyarthralgia is a frequent complaint and is usually of a 'rheumatoid' distribution. Rheumatoid factor is positive in 15–30% of cases; approximately one in ten patients with rheumatoid arthritis has evidence of fibrosing alveolitis. About one-third of patients do not have clubbed fingers.

ANF is positive in up to half of patients, but few of these have features of systemic lupus erythematosus. Many of the other 'collagen' diseases may be associated with fibrosing alveolitis including scleroderma, Sjögren's syndrome, dermatomyositis, Raynaud's phenomena, chronic active hepatitis etc.

57. Extrinsic allergic alveolitis   Answers: DE

Extrinsic allergic alveolitis occurs in atopic and non-atopic patients, with fever and constitutional upset being common in the acute phase.

Psittacosis is an acute pneumonia caused by *Chlamydia psittaci*. This is different from bird fancier's lung which is a type of extrinsic allergic alveolitis. The immunology is complex, but type III hypersensitivity with precipitin and immune complex formation is characteristic. Atopic people may have type I reactions but eosinophilia is unusual. Farmer's lung is a hypersensitivity reaction to *Micropolyspora faeni* and *Thermoactinomyces bulgaris* found in mouldy hay.

58. Aspergillosis   Answers: BE

When *Aspergillus* species colonise lung cavities caused by previous tuberculosis or other cavitating lung diseases, an aspergilloma is formed. Unless the patient is also allergic to *Aspergillus*, eosinophilia and positive skin test to *Aspergillus* are uncommon but *Aspergillus* precipitins are almost always present in serum.

In bronchocentric granulomatosis there is granulomata in the bronchial epithelium, but without the blood vessel involvement that occurs in, for example, Wegener's granulomatosis. There is a group with asthma and one without. The asthma group are younger and have blood eosinophilia, fungal elements in mucous plugs and aspergillus precipitins may be positive.

Allergic bronchopulmonary aspergillosis is a type of asthma with eosinophilic pulmonary infiltrates in which serum precipitins to *Aspergillus* are positive in 80% of patients. Proximal bronchiectasis is a common complication.

Intravenous amphotericin B is the treatment of choice at present in invasive aspergillosis but the mortality remains very high. Septrin is ineffective.

59. Legionnaires' disease   Answers: BCD

Inhalation of small contaminated water droplets into alveoli is the most common portal of entry in the disease and *Legionella pneumophila* may be isolated from many water sources. Shower units and air conditioning units have frequently been implicated. Rubber washers in taps and shower units may support growth with high concentrations being released when first used in the morning. No evidence exists for person to person infection.

Constitutional upset with high fever, rigors, myalgia, nausea, abdominal pain and diarrhoea is common. Microscopic haematuria is frequent.

Sputum, pleural fluid and blood cultures are occasionally positive but diagnosis is usually made by detection of antibodies by the indirect fluorescent antibody test.

60. Antituberculous chemotherapy   Answers: ADE

Isoniazid may cause a predominant sensory neuropathy but this is uncommon in normal doses (200–300 mg daily); it occurs in higher doses particularly in the undernourished. It may be prevented by giving pyridoxine.

A particular side-effect of ethambutol is retrobulbar neuritis, but this is uncommon particularly in doses of 15 mg/kg or less and for periods of up to 2 months in higher doses.

Bacillus-Calmette-Guérin (BCG) vaccine is an strain of *M. bovis* with extremely low virulence but high immune stimulation. Up to 10% of the population are atopic, but disseminated BCG infection occurs only in atopic patients with widespread eczema. It also occurs in patients who are immunosuppressed.

Rifampicin causes the urine to be stained orange/brown. Pyrazinamide is a powerful drug to which resistance rapidly develops unless used in combination. Its major side-effect is hepatotoxicity and increased serum urate.

61. Pneumothorax   Answers: ABCE

Pneumothorax may occur in a number of the inherited collagen disorders such as Ehlers–Danlos, Marfan's and pseudoxanthoma elasticum. High inflation pressures and high levels of PEEP during IPPV predispose to pneumothoraces as can any cavitating lung disease, including tuberculosis, where a subpleural cavity may rupture into the pleural space.

Small left sided pneumothoraces may cause audible clicks often felt by the patient. They vary with position and inspiration and occur throughout the cardiac cycle. They are probably extra-cardiac in origin although spontaneous pneumothorax has been associated with mitral valve prolapse which may give systolic clicks.

In the acute phase, the patient with a moderate to large pneumothorax becomes hypoxic, probably due to shunting of blood through the collapsed, poorly ventilated lung. However, there is redistribution of blood flow and in the patient with otherwise 'normal' lungs the hypoxia is corrected. The patients show a restrictive defect in pulmonary function with a reduction in vital capacity, a proportionate reduction in FEV_1 and therefore a normal to high FEV_1/VC ratio.

62. Treatment of sarcoidosis   Answers: BD

Bilateral hilar lymphadenopathy is usually asymptomatic even when large. It does not require treatment. Erythema nodosum is usually mild with little constitutional upset and also requires no treatment. If symptoms are troublesome and recurrent and have not responded to non-steroidal anti-inflammatory drugs, steroids are occasionally indicated. In most cases the arthralgia of sarcoidosis is associated with erythema nodosum and is mild with no active arthritis. It usually requires only symptomatic measures.

In all cases of ocular sarcoidosis, systemic steroids should be employed to prevent permanent damage. They should also be given to patients with central nervous system involvement.

Generally, in sarcoidosis, corticosteroids are reserved for vital organ involvement and hypercalcaemia. They may be used for 'symptomatic' treatment in the unusual case where symptoms are recurrent and troublesome.

63. Normal chest radiograph
Answers: CDE

The right diaphragm is usually higher than the left, but in 10–15% of normal people the diaphragms are of equal height. The right diaphragm is usually at the level of the anterior end of the 6th rib on an inspiratory PA film.

The normal heart width is less than 50% of the maximum horizontal thoracic diameter (cardiothoracic ratio) and varies by about 1 cm in diameter through the cardiac cycle.

64. Occupational lung diseases
Answers: ABD

As well as pleural mesothelioma, exposure to relatively small amounts of asbestos has been implicated in causing the much rarer peritoneal mesothelioma.

The main group of people to develop progressive massive fibrosis (PMF) are coal miners. It may be due to contamination with silica or other mineral dusts.

Sensitivity to toluene di-isocyanate may develop and cause bronchospasm indistinguishable from asthma. Repeated exposure causes worsening of symptoms and fixed airways obstruction. Bronchospasm may persist for many weeks and months after removal from exposure.

Exposure to tin oxide dust (stannosis) may cause very dramatic X-ray appearances showing widespread mottling with highly radio-opaque material but the compound is non-irritant and causes no symptoms or pulmonary function abnormality.

65. Pulmonary hypertension
Answers: BC

The upper limits of pulmonary artery pressure are 30 mm Hg systolic, and 15 mm Hg mean. Levels above these suggest pulmonary hypertension.

Obliteration of the small pulmonary arteries by, for example *Schistosoma* ova or recurrent pulmonary emboli causes pulmonary hypertension. However, the commonest cause of pulmonary hypertension in Great Britain is chronic airflow obstruction due to chronic bronchitis.

Unless recent emboli can be identified in large or medium sized pulmonary arteries by pulmonary angiography, it is usually impossible to differentiate between primary pulmonary hypertension and recurrent pulmonary emboli at cardiac catheterisation. Lung biopsy may show the classical features of primary pulmonary hypertension with the dilated plexiform lesions in the muscular pulmonary arteries.

Gross obesity may be associated with hypoventilation and sleep related disorders of breathing which cause hypoxic pulmonary hypertension.

NEUROLOGY

66. Posterior columns of the spinal cord   Answers: CE

The posterior (dorsal) column of the spinal cord is composed mainly of large myelinated fibres originating in the ipsilateral dorsal root ganglia. Fibres from below the mid-thoracic region terminate in the nucleus gracilis, above this is the nucleus cuneatus. Projections from these decussate in the medulla before continuing as the medial lemniscus.

The blood supply to the dorsal columns is derived from the posterior spinal arteries arising from the vertebral or posterior cerebellar arteries and supplemented by the radicular arteries. The great artery of Adamkiewicz enters around T_{12} and augments the *anterior artery*. The anterior spinal artery syndrome often results from occlusion of this artery with paraparesis and loss of pain sensation below T_{12} but preservation of vibration and light touch.

The posterior columns transmit proprioception (Romberg's sign), light touch (together with the spino-thalamic tracts), vibration and deep pain.

Diseases particularly affecting the posterior columns include B_{12} neuropathy, tabes dorsalis, and pseudotabes occurring in diabetes mellitus. Pseudo-athetosis is seen in multiple sclerosis, where the damage to the posterior cord in the cervical region leads to severe loss of joint proprioception in the hands with the consequent development of pseudo-athetoid movements.

67. Hearing   Answers: ABE

The pathway for hearing arises in the organ of Corti, the cochlear, and the spiral ganglion. Fibres then travel in the auditory nerve to the one dorsal and two ventral nuclei on each side. From here fibres project through the lateral lemniscus with some decussation to the inferior colliculus and the medial geniculate body. The final common pathway is to the superior temporal gyrus. Some fibres also synapse in the superior olive nucleus.

Owing to the complex central organisation of the auditory pathway, clinically overt disturbances of hearing rarely result from discrete lesions of the brainstem or auditory cortex.

The tests of auditory function are complex and should include assessment of the vestibular portion of the VIII nerve. Loudness recruitment is of value in detecting patients with sensorineural deafness due to cochlear end-organ disease as in Ménière's syndrome. With increasing intensity of the stimulus the sound eventually seems equal in both the damaged and undamaged ears.

Tone decay is a feature of auditory nerve damage, in particular due to an acoustic neuroma. The intensity of sound presented to the affected ear has to be increased with time for it to appear unchanged (because of 'decay').

68. Lateral popliteal nerve   Answers: ABD

Questions about specific peripheral nerves occur in the exam. They are difficult to guess at the time; you need detailed knowledge of major nerves (ulnar, median, radial, sciatic, popliteals and femoral) including conditions that commonly cause damage to them. The lateral popliteal (common peroneal) is the smaller of the two terminal divisions of the sciatic nerve, the other being the medial popliteal nerve (tibial nerve). Its roots are L4,5, S1,2. It passes through the popliteal fossa winding around the head of the fibula close to the biceps femoris. Subsequently the nerve divides into the superficial and deep peroneal branches. It supplies peroneus longus and brevis (superficial branch) and tibialis anterior, extensor digitorum longus and brevis, extensor hallucis longus, and peroneus tertius (deep branch). The nerve also carries the sensory fibres from the lateral aspect of the lower limb including the ankle and dorsum of the foot.

Lesions of the lateral popliteal nerve produce foot drop, loss of eversion and toe extension, with sensory impairment as indicated above. Any condition causing a mononeuritis may injure the nerve, e.g. diabetes, polyarteritis nodosa, or SLE. Trauma/pressure is a common cause of foot drop. It can also be severely affected in the hereditary sensorimotor neuropathies (e.g. Charcot–Marie–Tooth).

69. Neurological anatomy and physiology   Answers: CDE

There are many neuronal cell types within the CNS. Betz's or pyramidal cells are found in the *pre-central* gyrus or motor cortex. Purkinje cells are located in the cerebellar cortex. The unipolar neurone is typical of the dorsal root ganglia and sensory ganglia of the cranial nerves. The bipolar neurone occurs in the cranial nerves for special senses.

The fibres of any nerve are composed of small unmyelinated 'c' fibres (conduction velocity 0.5–2.0 m/s, where an action potential is conducted by a spreading wave of depolarisation) increasing to the large 'a' fibres (70–120 m/s) in which the nerve impulse is conducted by 'jumping' along the nodes of Ranvier. 'C' fibres are the dominant type in the vagus comprising approximately 90% of the axons and are concerned with the transmission of noxious information.

Both the gamma motor neurone loop and the Golgi tendon organ are involved in the clasp knife reflex, which is classically seen in lesions of the pyramidal tract. When a muscle is stretched, activity within the gamma motor neurone loop is increased because of stimulation of the muscle spindles. If the applied force is great the discharge of the alpha motor neurone is strongly inhibited by impulses arising in the Golgi tendon organ and the muscle 'gives way' as in a clasp knife.

The centre for vertical gaze is situated in the midbrain unlike the centres for horizontal and downward gaze which are located in the brainstem. Lesions of the upper midbrain cause paresis of conjugate upward gaze often with loss of the pupillary light reflexes and convergence (Parinaud's syndrome). It can rarely be congenital, but is usually associated with encephalitis, tumours around the 3rd ventricle, midbrain, or pineal body, Wernicke's encephalopathy, or infarction.

70. Muscle spindles
Answers: BCD

Muscle spindles are found in all voluntary muscles, but are few in number in the extra-ocular muscles. Seven to eight fibres are contained in a capsule and termed *intrafusal*. The tension within these fibres is maintained through their innervation by gamma-motor neurones situated in the anterior horn of the spinal cord. There are sensory endings (annulospiral and flower spray) innervating the spindle. If these receptors are depolarised by stretching of the skeletal muscle then afferent impulses in small myelinated axons (groups IA,B) projecting to the dorsal roots of the spinal cord (through monosynaptic and polysynaptic connections) cause an increased discharge of the gamma-motor neurone and contraction to oppose the stretch of the extrafusal fibres.

If the gamma-motor neurone activity is increased then the contraction of the intrafusal fibres on the sensory endings causes an increased tension of the sensory endings and this in turn leads to heightened activity and tone within the skeletal muscle.

Golgi tendon receptors protect the muscle against increased stretch as in the clasp knife reflex. The stretch response is the basis of the tendon reflexes but not the cremasteric or abdominal reflexes which depend on skin sensory receptors and afferents.

Cog-wheel rigidity is found in disease of the extrapyramidal system (e.g. Parkinson's disease) where the tremor is superimposed on the lead-pipe or plastic rigidity.

71. Bladder function   Answer: B

The bladder is principally controlled by the parasympathetic outflow from the sacral centre (S2,3,4). Some sympathetic fibres innervate the trigone and urethra (both α-contraction, and β-relaxation receptors).

The anterior rami of the sacral nerves give off visceral branches and comprise the pelvic splanchnic nerves. The pudendal nerves arise from the same segments but supply the pelvic floor, perineum, scrotum (labia), penis (some parasympathetic fibres) and clitoris.

Bladder control is integrated in the sacral centre but is controlled from higher centres in the pons, midbrain, posterior hypothalamus and ultimately in the frontal lobe of the cerebral cortex.

Cholinergic stimulation leads to detrusor muscle and trigone contraction with increased intravesical pressure and funnelling/shortening of the upper part of the urethra.

Anticholinergic drugs (e.g. imipramine) can be useful in patients with an unstable (detrusor muscle) or uninhibited bladder.

72. Trigeminal nerve   Answer: E

Detailed knowledge is required of the anatomy of the cranial nerves and the conditions affecting them. The trigeminal nerve consists of a motor and sensory element. The motor nucleus lies in the pons; its outflow passes below the gasserian ganglion to join the mandibular division. It supplies the temporalis, masseters and pterygoid muscles (if the pterygoids are paralysed then the jaw deviates to that side).

The Vth nerve supplies the whole of the face from the vertex to just above the jawline. Innervation can extend to the pinna but it usually ceases at the angle of the jaw. The vertex is supplied by C2.

The sensory fibres project to the principal sensory nucleus in the upper pons. Fibres conveying pain and temperature turn down and pass through the medulla into the upper two or three cervical segments. They then decussate and become the ascending or quintothalamic tract.

The central organisation of the sensory innervation is in an 'onion skin' distribution with loss or dissociation starting over the angle of the jaw and cheek spreading across the face. This differs from the classical lesions affecting one of the peripheral divisions.

Particular conditions affecting the trigeminal nerve are herpes zoster, trigeminal neuralgia, compression by an acoustic neuroma, lesions around the cavernous sinus (where the 3rd division will be spared) and multiple sclerosis.

73. Dopaminergic pathways   Answer: E

There are three principal pathways of dopamine containing neurones: (i) the nigrostriatal system originates in the substantia nigra and projects to the basal ganglia (ii) the tubero-infundibular system involved in hypothalamic-pituitary control (iii) the mesolimbic system which arises in the midbrain and projects to the caudate, putamen, amygdala and olfactory tubercle.

The pathways are inhibitory, for example bromocriptine, a dopamine agonist, suppresses the release of prolactin.

Tyrosine, which is formed by the hydroxylation of phenylalanine, is converted by tyrosine hydroxylase into L-dopa. Decarboxylation of L-dopa produces dopamine. This can then be converted in the presence of oxygen and ascorbic acid to noradrenaline.

The degradation of dopamine depends on monoamine oxidase type B. Selegiline inhibits this breakdown. It became popular in the treatment of Parkinson's disease because of studies suggesting that it delayed progression of the disease. These studies have not been confirmed and there are concerns about an increase in mortality. A principal effect of selegiline is to improve mood (because of some inhibition of the Type A enzyme). The dose of L-dopa may have to be reduced if it is given concurrently with selegiline.

74. Substance P   Answer: B

Substance P is a polypeptide. It is found in the myenteric plexus of the intestine, the spinal cord and hypothalamus and substantia nigra.

Its major function appears to be in modifying pain as impulses are transmitted through the dorsal roots, substantia gelatinosa and the spino-thalamic tract.

The mechanism of action of sodium valproate is in enhancing the action of γ-aminobutyric acid (GABA) which is a major inhibitory neurotransmitter.

Aspartic and glutamic acid (amino acids), as with substance P, are excitatory transmitters. GABA and glycine are inhibitory. Uncontrolled release of aspartate and glutamate following brain injury (including stroke) leads to influx of calcium into neurones and cell death. There are a number of drugs under development that block aspartate receptors and act as neuro-protective agents.

75. The treatment of spasticity   Answers: CE

Diazepam, baclofen and dantrolene sodium can be used in the treatment of spasticity together with destructive procedures such as injections of phenol (rarely used). All produce muscle weakness to some extent and this has to be weighed against benefit.

Baclofen penetrates the blood–brain barrier poorly, it is therefore a very potent drug. The dose has to be titrated against weakness and side-effects such as confusion, hypotonia, fatigue and drowsiness. It acts mainly at the spinal level, possibly through mimicking the actions of GABA, and is very useful in patients with flexor spasms. Abrupt withdrawal can precipitate visual hallucinations, convulsions and cardiac arrhythmias.

Diazepam may be of benefit as a muscle relaxant in the absence of excess sedation. Its actions within the cord are probably due to an agonist effect at glycine receptors.

Dantrolene sodium acts by inhibiting the release of calcium from the sarcoplasmic reticulum thereby producing a dissociation of excitation-contraction coupling. The major side-effect is hepatotoxicity where, in the presence of pre-existing liver disease, an acute hepatitis, chronic active hepatitis or cirrhosis may occur.

76. Nystagmus   Answers: AC

A number of 'rules' govern the analysis of nystagmus:(i) it is always named according to the direction of the fast movement; (ii) the amplitude of the nystagmus is greatest when looking in the direction of the fast movement; (iii) in a peripheral lesion the fast movement is away, whereas in a central problem the movement is towards.

Occasionally the patient is aware of nystagmus especially in the acute phase (oscillopsia).

In ataxic nystagmus the lesion is in the medial longitudinal bundle connecting the VIth nerve (leading eye) to the IIIrd nerve (following eye). Thus, in ataxic nystagmus the abducting eye moves laterally with coarse nystagmus, but the adducting eye fails to move medially and fine nystagmus may be present. Ataxic nystagmus is almost pathognomonic of multiple sclerosis, but vascular conditions, diabetes mellitus, tumours and encephalitis may cause a similar problem.

Downbeat nystagmus, where the direction of the movement is down, is characteristic of pathology around the foramen magnum. Nystagmus in a vertical plane only occurs in central lesions.

Benign positional vertigo only induces nystagmus in a horizontal direction, and the symptoms can be reproduced by turning the head suddenly when the patient is laid flat and the head extended 30 degrees (Hallpike manoeuvre). If the test is repeated, nystagmus does not recur as adaptation takes place quickly. The affected ear needs to be the lowest.

77. Normal pressure hydrocephalus   Answer: B

Normal pressure hydrocephalus (NPH) is a disorder usually of unknown aetiology (50%) but can be associated with head injury, subarachnoid haemorrhage, intracranial surgery, encephalitis or cerebrovascular disease. The classical triad of symptoms comprise dementia, urinary incontinence and unsteadiness of gait. Occasionally, Parkinsonian features may be found.

In many series the only reasonable predictors of response to a shunt were the presence of a gait disorder and urinary incontinence in the absence of dementia. The duration of the symptoms did not influence the outcome.

No reliable single objective measurement has been devised. Neither the ventricular size nor the ratio of sulcal dilatation to ventricular diameter is of proven value. The most promising screening procedure is long term pressure monitoring to detect the pressure waves which occur in NPH, but not in ventricular dilatation secondary to brain atrophy.

Only about half of patients subjected to a shunt procedure will make a good response. Major complications encountered are subdural collections of fluid and shunt infection with ventriculitis.

78. Carotid stenosis   Answers: AD

The relationship of bruits to carotid stenoses is not simple, but most patients with a severe stenosis have a bruit. The danger of relying on auscultation is a false negative result (i.e. missing a severe stenosis); all patients with TIAs or minor strokes in a carotid territory should have duplex ultrasound examination.

The ECST and the NASCET studies have shown clear benefit to symptomatic patients with >70% stenosis. If the stenosis is less than this, the risks outweigh the benefits (low annual stroke rate).

The annual risk of stroke will be around 10% per year depending on risk factors present.

In the best centres, the risk of death or major stroke at the time of the operation is 2–3%. In most centres, the average is around 5%.

Altitudinous hemianopia affects only the ipsilateral eye in the superior or inferior field of vision. It is a form of amaurosis fugax.

79. Subarachnoid haemorrhage   Answers: AC

Subarachnoid haemorrhage (SAH) untreated carries a mortality of approximately 45% in the first 8 weeks. A major cause of morbidity is rebleeding which is at its peak at 7–14 days and occurs in 30–40% of all patients surviving the initial episode. A further serious problem is cerebral vasospasm which is probably related to the amount of blood within the CSF and appears in the territory of the vessel with the aneurysm. Occasionally it is widespread and carries a serious prognosis. It may be exacerbated by angiography.

The early use of nimodipine has reduced the mortality significantly.

10% of patients who bleed do so from an angioma. In 15–20% the aneurysms are multiple. In up to 25% of the remainder no source of the bleeding will be found even at post mortem.

A common site of aneurysm formation is the posterior communicating artery where an expanding or leaking aneurysm may compress the 3rd nerve.

A CT scan will show blood in the CSF in at least 90% of cases scanned within 7 days. Owing to the risk of coning, a lumber puncture should be avoided if possible. Serial scans show a mild hydrocephalus in up to 20% of patients within 14 days. A much smaller proportion develop clinically overt communicating hydrocephalus.

80. Eye movements   Answers: ACDE

When analysing eye movements remember that the muscles act in pairs with the obliques acting as elevators (inferior) or depressors (superior) of the globe when the eye is adducted and the inferior and superior recti acting when the eye is abducted.

Centres for voluntary fixation are situated in both frontal lobes. If the left frontal lobe is stimulated (e.g. epilepsy) the eyes turn away from that side and if damaged (e.g. stroke) the eyes turn toward the lesion and hence away from the hemiparetic side. The pathways then descend and cross to further centres within the midbrain and brainstem. A stroke in the brain stem will have the opposite effect of making the patient look towards the hemiparesis.

In progressive supranuclear palsy (Steele-Richardson-Olswesky syndrome) voluntary downward gaze is severely affected with subsequent involvement of gaze in all directions. Eventually involuntary fixation is also damaged with loss of the accommodation reflex. The patient is ultimately rendered rigid (extrapyramidal) with an extended posture particularly of the head.

In both Parkinson's disease and Huntington's chorea, upward gaze can be affected. Eye movement disorder including oculogyric crises are characteristic of postencephalitic Parkinsonism.

81. Oligoclonal bands in the CSF   Answers: ABCDE

The protein found within the CSF is derived partly by filtration of serum, partly from brain interstitial fluid and partly from cells of the CSF. If the blood–brain barrier breaks down, as in meningitis, the protein content rises due to leakage of plasma proteins (predominantly albumin). Hence the globulin (a large protein) to albumin ratio remains small.

If an excess amount of immunoglobulins is produced intrathecally as part of an immune response then the globulin to albumin ratio will increase and reflect this production. An oligoclonal band of gamma globulin (often IgG) will be detected in the protein electrophoresis.

An oligoclonal immune response is a hallmark of established multiple sclerosis. However, the percentage of patients having a band at the stage when the disease is suspected is less than 50%, only increasing as the disease progresses. The best diagnostic test is MR imaging.

Other conditions where a band has been described are neurosyphilis, subacute sclerosing panencephalitis (antibody to measles virus), meningitis, encephalitis, systemic lupus erythematosus, Guillain–Barré syndrome, sarcoidosis and tumours.

A monoclonal band may appear in the CSF of patients with multiple myeloma, lymphoma, or benign paraproteinaemia. If the CNS is involved the protein may occur in larger quantities than in the plasma.

82. Multiple sclerosis   Answers: BE

The diagnosis of multiple sclerosis (MS) is a predominantly clinical one requiring discrete lesions in time and space. Investigations only aid in confirming your suspicion. Magnetic resonance imaging has become the investigation of choice. Using gadolinium, the age of plaques can be estimated (recent plaques enhance), confirming previous neurological damage. Visual evoked potentials can be measured and are abnormal even in the absence of previous optic neuritis. Examination of the CSF may show, in an acute relapse, a mild rise in protein and lymphocytosis.

Both hemianopia and dysphasia are extremely rare manifestations of MS. Epilepsy is more common, occurring in approximately 5% as a late complication. Red and green colour impairment or dimming of vision are common sequelae of optic neuritis.

Bad prognostic signs are being male, onset after 40 years, predominant motor signs, poor recovery between each relapse and a short interval between each episode.

Corticosteroids reduce the time interval to recovering whatever function is possible after each relapse. The interferons (α, β) may reduce relapse and (possibly) disability in some patients.

83. Subacute combined degeneration of the spinal cord   Answers: BDE

Subacute combined degeneration of the spinal cord (SACD) due to vitamin B_{12} deficiency may occur in the absence of anaemia or rarely macrocytosis.

Other manifestations include optic atrophy and fever. Dementia does occur, but rarely and almost always the cord disease is very severe.

The brunt of the damage falls on the dorsal root ganglia with loss of the large sensory afferents and their projections within the posterior columns. Pathologically, extensive changes are found in the thoracic cord. Thus, B_{12} deficiency may present solely as a severe peripheral neuropathy with absent tendon and plantar reflexes.

The corticospinal tracts can also be affected with pyramidal signs alone or in combination with a peripheral neuropathy.

Only in severe cases are the arms and hands involved.

Treatment will halt the progression of the disease and there may be some recovery, but it is often partial if the diagnosis is made late.

84. Nerve supply of the upper limb   Answers: ABE

The posterior interosseus nerve is the continuation of the radial nerve in the forearm after triceps, brachioradialis and the extensor carpi radialis have been supplied. It innervates the muscles of the posterior compartment including the long extensors of the fingers, and the thumb. It also gives branches to supinator and abductor pollicis longus (not brevis - median).

The root supply of the muscles of the hand is predominantly T1 with some fibres from C8.

In the forearm the median nerve supplies pronator teres, flexor carpi radialis, palmaris longus and flexor digitorum superficialis. The anterior branch innervates half of flexor digitorum profundus, flexor pollicis longus and pronator quadratus.

The palmar (adduction) and dorsal (abduction) interossei are supplied by the ulnar nerve. The lumbricals (I and II, median) flex the fingers at the metacarpophalangeal joints.

85. Dementia   Answer: E

The incidence of multi-infarct dementia varies from 10 to 30% in any series. This is undoubtedly due to the lack of a good differentiation test between this and Alzheimer's disease.

If a gait disturbance or urinary incontinence appears early in the course of a dementing illness, normal pressure hydrocephalus should be considered. The presence of any symptoms or signs which may arise from subcortical structures should alert the clinician to diagnoses other than the pure cortical dementias (e.g. Wilson's disease, Huntington's chorea, or Parkinson's disease).

Pick's disease is a very rare condition which may be differentiated from Alzheimer's dementia by the relative lack of parietal signs, memory loss and anomia in the face of severe behavioural disturbances. The CT scan may be helpful in showing localised atrophy in the frontal and temporal lobes.

The rapid progression of a dementing process with associated long tract signs, myoclonic jerks and severe rigidity point to Jakob-Creutzfeldt disease. An EEG is abnormal in approximately 90% of cases showing characteristic changes. An LP or CT scan is unhelpful.

86. Muscle fasciculation Answers: ABE

Muscle fasciculations are irregular contractions of muscle fibres that are innervated by the same motor unit. They are caused by irregular firing of anterior horn cells or an irritative focus in the peripheral nerve.

They are often seen in sub-acute or acute denervation.

Causes include motor neurone disease, acute poliomyelitis, spinal root disease (e.g. cervical spondylosis), thyrotoxicosis, severe hyponatraemia, hypomagnesaemia, generalised polyneuropathies and with certain drugs (anticholinesterase, lithium).

87. Cerebral damage Answers: BCD

All sensory input to the cortex passes through the posterior limb of the internal capsule.

Gerstmann's syndrome consists of acalculia, agraphia, impaired right–left discrimination and finger agnosia and is caused by a lesion in the dominant angular gyrus.

Parietal lobe damage manifests as a defect of inattention in the contralateral visual field, astereognosis, constructional apraxia (non-dominant), prosopagnosia (inability to recognise familiar faces, non-dominant), dressing apraxia (non-dominant), Gerstmann's syndrome (dominant) and ideomotor apraxia (dominant).

The frontal lobes play a major role in personality and the planning and initiation of action. The continence centre is located here.

Occipital damage frequently produces homonymous hemianopia with macular sparing. Quadrantic hemianopias are produced by lesions in the temporal lobe (superior - most common) or parietal lobe (inferior).

88. CSF   Answer: A

The brain is covered by the meninges, which consist of the thick dura mater externally, the arachnoid lining the dura and the pia mater adherent to the brain and spinal cord. The arachnoid and the pia are the boundaries of the subarachnoid space which is filled by the cerebrospinal fluid (CSF).

The CSF is produced at a constant rate of about 450 ml/day by the choroid plexuses of the lateral (most important), third and fourth ventricles. Flow is from the lateral ventricles into the third ventricle and then the fourth ventricle by way of the aqueduct. Foramina allow drainage from the fourth ventricle into the pontine cistern and cisterna magna. Blockage along this route may cause a non-communicating hydrocephalus. Causes of blockage include tumour or blood within the ventricular system.

The CSF flows through the cisternal spaces and over the cerebral hemispheres. Absorption into the dural venous sinuses is through the arachnoid villi. Blockage here, for example by blood from a subarachnoid haemorrhage may cause a communicating hydrocephalus.

The CSF volume is around 80–200 ml with a recumbent pressure between 80 and 180 ml of water. You must know the approximate normal values for CSF constituents. Key values are:

Protein   0.25–0.50 g/l
Glucose *   2.5–5.5 mmol/l
White cells   <5 cells (lymphocytes)/mm^3
Red cells**   0

* This is dependent on the blood glucose value (it should be 50–70% – consider the effect of diabetes mellitus).
** Should be zero. A 'bloody tap' may contaminate the fluid.

89. Action potential of the neurone   **Answers: AE**

The action potential is an all-or-none phenomenon principally caused by the opening of fast sodium channels and the influx of sodium into the cell, making the inside more positive and depolarising the cell.

The impulse propagates bidirectionally.

Large sensory fibres can conduct at extremely fast rates (>60 m/s). The speed is dependent on the axon size and degree of myelination.

ENDOCRINOLOGY

90. Addison's disease
Answer: B

It is unsafe to rely on basal serum cortisol concentration which may be normal in some patients with Addison's disease. The adrenal response to ACTH stimulation should be studied to assess adrenocortical reserve.

Salt depletion leads to postural hypotension. The reduced intravascular volume with reduced renal perfusion usually leads to an elevated blood urea concentration.

Anorexia, nausea and diarrhoea may all contribute to the weight loss that is characteristic of Addison's disease.

Addison's disease is much rarer than thyrotoxicosis. The commonest cause of Addison's disease is autoimmune adrenal disease and adrenocortical antibodies are found in a high proportion of patients.

91. Thyrotoxicosis
Answers: ABD

Hyperthyroidism may be associated with an elevated serum T_3 concentration and a normal serum thyroxine concentration.

Hyperthyroidism increases the serum sex hormone binding globulin (SHBG) level and thus the circulating free oestrogen:androgen ratio.

Graves' disease is caused by circulating thyroid stimulating immunoglobulins, which are antibodies against the TSH receptor on the thyroid cell.

Patients with thyrotoxicosis are often nervous, emotionally labile and hyperkinetic. Fatigue may be a manifestation of muscle weakness and insomnia, which is common. In certain patients the features of lethargy and depression (apathetic thyrotoxicosis) may be prominent.

The reverse T_3 in serum is present almost entirely due to generation from thyroxine (T_4) in the peripheral tissues. Consequently the quantity of T_4 available is an important determinant of the serum reverse T_3 concentration so that it rises in thyrotoxicosis and declines in hypothyroidism.

92. Thyroid carcinoma   Answers: BC

The most common histological type of thyroid cancer is papillary and the second commonest is follicular. Typically, papillary thyroid carcinoma occurs in young people and anaplastic in elderly people. Both papillary and medullary thyroid carcinoma (MTC) occur in childhood.

On clinical examination, a solitary thyroid lump in a patient with hyperthyroidism is rarely a thyroid malignancy. A toxic adenoma, coincidental benign cyst or multinodular goitre are much more likely diagnoses.

Neck irradiation in childhood, which exposes the thyroid gland to a radiation dose between a few cGy (rads) to 2000 cGy may predispose to the development of thyroid carcinoma some 30 years later. A greater radiation dose is more likely to cause hypothyroidism.

A raised calcitonin concentration is a biochemical marker for MTC. However, it does not cause hypocalcaemia. Indeed hypercalcaemia may be associated with MTC due to co-existent hyperparathyroidism (Multiple endocrine adenomatosis type 2).

93. Bromocriptine   Answer: C

Bromocriptine is a semi-synthetic ergot alkaloid derivative that acts as a dopamine agonist and consequently reduces the circulating prolactin level in both normal and hyperprolactinaemic subjects. Therefore, it is very effective in suppressing puerperal lactation.

It stimulates growth hormone secretion in normal subjects and reduces growth hormone levels in a proportion of acromegalic subjects.

The commonest side-effects are nausea, vomiting and dizziness. Tolerance rapidly develops to these symptoms. The drug should initially be prescribed in low dosage and taken with meals. Other problems include postural hypotension, nightmares and confusional psychotic states.

The other main use is in the treatment of Parkinson's disease where it can be used alone or in combination with other drugs including L-dopa. There are other dopaminergic agonists such as pergolide.

94. Phaeochromocytoma   Answers: ACE

Phaeochromocytoma is occasionally inherited as an autosomal dominant trait and may be part of multiple endocrine adenomatosis (MEA) type 2 (phaeochromocytoma, medullary thyroid carcinoma and hyperparathyroidism). Familial phaeochromocytomas are more often bilateral than the sporadic form. About 5% of reported cases of phaeochromocytoma have associated neurofibromatosis (Recklinghausen's syndrome). About 6–10% of adrenal phaeochromocytomas are malignant, as determined by either local invasion or metastases. Malignancy cannot be determined by histological appearance alone.

Although the paroxysmal episodes are the most distinctive manifestation of phaeochromocytoma, hypertension is the most common feature, occurring in over 90% of patients. It is usually sustained.

Phaeochromocytoma may resemble thyrotoxicosis. Similarities include nervous irritability, eyelid retraction, tremulousness, excessive sweating and tachycardia. In a patient with phaeochromocytoma, goitre is absent and, with rare exceptions, the thyroid function tests are normal.

95. Cushing's syndrome with bronchial carcinoma   Answers: CD

The production of ACTH-like peptides by a bronchial carcinoma is responsible for an ectopic syndrome. The secretion of the hormone by the carcinoma is not influenced by normal physiological control mechanisms. Therefore, dexamethasone does not reduce the circulating ACTH level and cortisol secretion.

The survival of patients with bronchial carcinoma is usually too brief to allow the clinical manifestations of Cushing's syndrome to appear. Hypokalaemic alkalosis is the predominant biochemical feature of classical ectopic ACTH production. The mechanism is ill-understood but recent evidence suggests that the higher molecular weight forms of ACTH, which are often secreted by these tumours may stimulate the adrenocortical secretion of mineralocorticoids to a greater extent compared with any given level of authentic 1–39 ACTH.

Whilst, as a group, patients with ectopic ACTH have higher plasma ACTH levels than those with pituitary-dependent disease, there is considerable overlap. However, extremely high basal ACTH levels are usually associated with clinically overt tumours such as small cell carcinoma of the bronchus.

96. Acromegaly   Answer: D

Growth hormone (GH) release may be induced by stress. Therefore, a high random serum growth hormone level does not confirm acromegaly. A glucose tolerance test is required with GH levels to demonstrate that the GH secretion fails to suppress to within the defined normal range after a glucose load.

A raised serum phosphate level is found in approximately 25% of acromegalics. GH increases phosphate reabsorption by the kidney.

Somatomedin C (IGF-1) is a growth hormone dependent growth-related peptide predominantly produced by the liver. The serum somatomedin C level is raised in acromegaly and reduced in GH deficiency.

Patients with acromegaly and carcinoid tumours have been described, in whom the carcinoid tumour has produced growth hormone releasing factor (GRF) identical to the naturally occurring hypothalamic GRF. Excision of the carcinoid tumour will lead to cure of the acromegaly.

Untreated acromegaly is associated with a considerable reduction in life expectancy. The excess mortality is attributed to cardiovascular disease, respiratory disease and diabetes mellitus.

97. Hyperprolactinaemia in the female   Answers: BCE

Hyperprolactinaemia in the female usually causes amenorrhoea or oligomenorrhoea. Rarely, it may be associated with regular menses and luteal dysfunction or even a completely normal menstrual cycle. In women with hyperprolactinaemia the commonest causes are a prolactin-secreting microadenoma (normal size pituitary fossa) or 'functional' hyperprolactinaemia. Most prolactin-secreting microadenomas do not develop into macroadenomas.

Increased secretion of prolactin, decreased clearance and a disparity between bioactive and immunoreactive serum prolactin concentrations occur in chronic renal failure.

Dopamine is the major prolactin inhibitory factor produced by the hypothalamus and prolactin secretion is under predominantly inhibitory control. Metoclopramide is a dopamine antagonist and its use will lead to hyperprolactinaemia.

Hyperprolactinaemia diminishes gonadotrophin pulsatility which leads to oestrogen deficiency in a proportion of patients. The latter may give rise to osteoporosis.

98. Gynaecomastia   Answers: AC

Either a decrease in the circulating free testosterone concentration or an increase in the free oestradiol concentration may lead to gynaecomastia.

Hyperprolactinaemia in the male may lead to loss of libido, impotence and sometimes galactorrhoea. Gynaecomastia is rare. Klinefelter's syndrome is a recognised cause of gynaecomastia. However it is associated with hypergonadotrophic not hypogonadotrophic hypogonadism.

In low doses, spironolactone is believed to cause gynaecomastia by inhibiting androgen binding. At higher concentrations, testosterone synthesis is inhibited. Other drug-induced causes of gynaecomastia apart from the sex hormones include digoxin, ethionamide, griseofulvin, reserpine, phenothiazines, imipramine and methyldopa.

In the vast majority of boys with pubertal gynaecomastia, the condition resolves spontaneously within 18 months.

99. Puberty   Answer: A

Menarche is a late event in puberty. On average there is only 2 inches (5cm) of growth potential remaining after menarche. The pubertal growth spurt in normal girls always occurs earlier.

Delayed pubertal development is most commonly due to physiological delay in development, hallmarked by short stature, delayed adrenarche, delayed gonadarche and a retarded bone age.

The commonest cause of central precocious puberty in girls is 'idiopathic'. In boys the commonest cause is a CNS lesion.

Cyproterone acetate which is used in hypersexuality acts as an anti-androgen at tissue level (e.g. skin) and suppresses gonadotrophin secretion by the hypothalamic–pituitary axis. If used in children, care must be taken with bone maturation. Side-effects include liver problems, thromboembolism, gynaecomastia, tiredness and weight gain.

100. Hypothyroidism   Answers: ABDE

In a thyroid gland that is failing, the serum T_3 level may remain in the normal range although the serum T_4 level is reduced and serum TSH level elevated. Eventually the serum T_3 level may also fall into the subnormal range.

In hyperthyroidism, hyperprolactinaemia may occur, giving rise to galactorrhoea and amenorrhoea. Restoration of a normal prolactin level and abolition of symptoms may be achieved with thyroxine replacement therapy.

Infiltration of subcutaneous tissues with mucopolysaccharides causes typical facial puffiness, ankle swelling and carpal tunnel syndrome, the last by compression of the median nerve within the flexor retinaculum of the wrist. Other causes of carpal tunnel syndrome include pregnancy, obesity, rheumatoid arthritis, acromegaly, and amyloidosis.

Pretibial myxoedema is a feature of Graves' disease and is frequently associated with eye signs such as exophthalmos. It occurs in less than 1% of thyrotoxic patients.

The macrocytosis occurs in isolation but there is a high incidence of pernicious anaemia in patients with primary hypothyroidism. Both frequent menorrhagia and defective absorption of iron resulting from achlorhydria may lead to a microcytic hypochromic anaemia.

101. Thyroiditis   Answers: BD

Hashimoto's thyroiditis is usually associated with a high titre of thyroid microsomal antibodies and thyroglobulin antibodies. Thyroid stimulating immunoglobulins are *only* present if there is co-existent Graves' disease.

In Turner's syndrome there is an increased incidence of Hashimoto's thyroiditis, which may result in hypothyroidism. Therefore thyroid function should be evaluated in every girl with Turner's syndrome to detect a treatable cause of short stature.

Typically patients with subacute thyroiditis may pass through a hyperthyroid phase due to release of preformed hormone by a damaged thyroid. This is followed by a hypothyroid phase associated with impaired synthesis of thyroid hormones and then recovery to a euthyroid state.

In some patients with sub-acute thyroiditis, the mumps virus has been implicated but Coxsackie, influenza, echoviruses and adenoviruses may also be aetiological agents. Apart from painful enlargement of the thyroid and a raised ESR, sub-acute thyroiditis is associated with a very low radio-iodine uptake, which is due to the inflammatory damage occurring in the thyroid gland.

102. Androgen physiology   Answers: AE

The Leydig cells in the testes produce more than 95% of the circulating androgens in man. The cells are under the control of luteinizing hormone (LH) whose release in turn is stimulated by luteiniting hormone-releasing hormone. The adrenal cortex secretes a small amount of androgen in response to ACTH. The prostate itself can metabolise testosterone precursors from the adrenals to the active hormone (may be up to 40% of total androgen stimulation of the gland).

Cyproterone acetate is a prostagenic anti-androgen which competes at testosterone receptors. Unwanted effects include impotence, fluid retention and gynaecomastia.

The gonadotrophin releasing hormone analogues initially *stimulate* luteiniting hormone release but then reduce LH and testosterone to levels similar to those found after castration. When used in prostatic cancer, they may produce a temporary disease 'flare'.

103. TSH   Answers: ACE

TSH is a glycoprotein made up of an α and β chain.

Together with LH, FSH and HCG the α units are all similar but the β chain confers specificity. The action on the thyroid is due to increased cAMP levels.

Metoclopropamide (a dopamine antagonist) may cause prolactin release.

METABOLIC MEDICINE

104. Diabetes mellitus   Answers: ABC

Chlorpropamide is a sulphonylurea drug that apart from its action on the pancreas, stimulates ADH secretion from the hypothalamus. It has been used in the treatment of partial diabetes insipidus. It is rarely used for new treatment because of its long half-life.

Profound sensory neuropathy may lead to the development of Charcot's joints, typically the feet and ankles.

Vitiligo may be associated with a number of auto-immune endocrinopathies such as diabetes mellitus, thyroid disease, Addison's disease, and premature gonadal failure.

Necrobiosis lipoidica diabeticorum is a skin manifestation of diabetes mellitus which typically affects young women on the shins.

There are three amino acid differences between beef and human insulins and one amino acid difference between porcine and human insulins. Antibody formation is greatest with beef insulin and least with human insulin. There is no evidence that human insulin is associated with greater frequency/severity of hypoglycaemic attacks or reduced warning.

105. Hypercalcaemia   Answers: CDE

Secondary hyperparathyroidism is a state of compensatory hypersecretion of parathormone (PTH) and may occur in any clinical condition in which there is a tendency toward hypocalcaemia (e.g. renal disease, malabsorption).

Pseudohypoparathyroidism is characterised by hypocalcaemia, hyperphosphataemia, a blunted phosphaturic response to exogenous PTH and a characteristic physical appearance, including short stature, round face, reduced intelligence and shortening of the metacarpals and metatarsals.

Vitamin D excess leads to hypercalcaemia by increasing both intestinal calcium absorption and bone resorption.

Thyrotoxicosis is associated with reduced intestinal calcium absorption, hypercalciuria, increased bone resorption and occasionally hypercalcaemia, which is usually mild.

Hypercalcaemia may occur as frequently in untreated Addison's disease as hyponatraemia and hyperkalaemia. Both decreased renal clearance of calcium and increased influx of calcium from bone to extracellular fluid have been observed.

Other important causes include malignancy (commonest aetiology in hospital, particularly myeloma), sarcoidosis, milk alkali syndrome and immobilisation in Paget's disease.

106. Hypoglycaemia   Answers: BCDE

The major action of metformin is to increase the peripheral utilisation of glucose. It does not cause hypoglycaemia either in normal subjects or in diabetics. In contrast sulphonylurea drugs stimulate the β-cells of the pancreatic islets to secrete more insulin. Hypoglycaemia may be a complication.

Hypoglycaemia is most common when hepatic destruction is both rapid and massive (e.g. in toxic hepatitis). It has been reported in fulminant viral hepatitis as in paracetamol poisoning, but is unusual in the common forms of cirrhosis and hepatitis.

In Addison's disease, the absence of glucocorticoids may lead to hypoglycaemia.

Multiple endocrine adenomatosis type 1 is characterised by pituitary tumours, pancreatic tumours and hyperparathyroidism. One type of pancreatic tumour seen is an insulinoma.

107. Hypokalaemia   Answers: ABC

Serum potassium usually parallels total body potassium, but it will also be affected by factors that specifically alter its distribution in the body such as acid–base state.

Hypokalaemia may be due to: (i) poor intake (rare); (ii) vomiting, where the resultant volume depletion leads to increased aldosterone production and a metabolic alkalosis, both of which induce renal potassium wasting; (iii) diarrhoea, where there is genuine faecal loss; (iv) renal potassium wasting (most common).

Renal potassium loss is indicated by a urinary excretion greater than 30 mmol/day in the presence of hypokalaemia. It is usually due to increased sodium delivery to the distal tubule caused by diuretics. It is also a feature of mineralocorticoid excess (e.g. aldosterone in Conn's syndrome and adrenal hyperplasia and non-aldosterone adrenal hormones in Cushing's syndrome and the adrenogenital syndromes).

Hyperkalaemia is a feature of hypoaldosteronism e.g. primary in Addison's disease or secondary in inappropriate hypoaldosteronism (hyporeninaemica hypoaldosteronism). It also occurs in systemic acidosis, with 'potassium sparing' diuretics and due to impaired excretion in renal failure.

Bartter's syndrome is characterised by hypersecretion of renin, secondary hyperaldosteronism, hypokalaemia and acidosis. Blood pressure is normal and oedema is absent. Renal biopsy shows juxtaglomerular hyperplasia. The pathogenesis is obscure, but many patients have a defect in the renal conservation of sodium with consequent salt wasting and hyponatraemia. It occurs most frequently in children and adolescents.

108. Metabolic acidosis   Answers: BCD

Metabolic acid–base disturbances are determined by a rise or fall in plasma bicarbonate concentration. Respiratory acid–base disturbances are characterised by abnormal blood PCO_2.

Respiratory compensation for metabolic disorders takes 6–12 hours. Renal compensation for respiratory disorders takes 3–5 days.

A normal anion gap (hyperchloraemic metabolic acidosis) will result when bicarbonate loss (from kidney i.e. type II renal tubule acidosis or from gut e.g. diarrhoea or pancreatic/biliary drainage) or failure of hydrogen ion secretion (e.g. distal renal tubular acidosis) is accompanied by chloride ion retention.

An elevated anion gap (normal gap is 10–14 mEq) develops when the anion of the generated acid is not rapidly excreted and therefore there is no chloride retention. The resulting normochloraemic metabolic acidosis occurs (e.g. in lactic acidosis, ketoacidosis, methanol and ethylene glycol poisoning).

Treatment is aimed at the primary condition. Bicarbonate therapy may be indicated for hyperkalaemia or if blood pH is less than 7.1.

109. Hypermagnesaemia   Answers: AB

Symptomatic hypermagnesaemia is a rare clinical condition which is usually iatrogenic. It may occur with magnesium overload in renal failure. Occasionally it is found if magnesium salts are administered rectally in patients with colonic disease. Intravenous and rectal magnesium sulphate are used in the treatment of pre-eclamptic toxaemia. Elevated magnesium levels have been reported in hypothyroidism, lithium therapy and the milk alkali syndrome.

The symptoms of hypermagnesaemia are usually apparent at levels above 2 mmol/l. Initially they comprise nausea and flushing. Subsequently, depression of the neuromuscular junction occurs with reduced muscle tone and tendon reflexes, drowsiness and paralysis (including the respiratory muscles). Hypotension occurs with bradycardia and eventually asystole.

Hypomagnesaemia is much more common, being found in chronic alcoholism, diabetic ketoacidosis, excessive losses or malabsorption from the gastrointestinal tract, treatment with diuretics and various endocrine states (primary aldosteronism, hyperthyroidism, and hyperparathyroidism).

Hypomagnesaemia is almost always accompanied by hypocalcaemia. Resistant hypokalaemia may also be seen. The most common features are paraesthesiae, cramps and tetany. Fits and other evidence of neuromuscular irritability may be apparent. Arrythmias occur including ventricular tachycardia and fibrillation.

110. Parathormone control   Answers: ABE

Parathormone (PTH) is an 84 amino-acid molecule that is manufactured by the chief cells of the parathyroid glands. This is cleaved both within the gland and in the Kupffer's cells into a 1–34 amino-acid fragment, (which is biologically active and has a very short half-life) and the C-terminal fragment. The latter is inactive and is cleared more slowly by the kidney.

The secretion of PTH is stimulated by a fall in serum calcium and suppressed by hypercalcaemia. A similar relationship exists with magnesium except in chronic depletion where there is loss of secretion and decreased end-organ responsiveness.

PTH directly inhibits the reabsorption of phosphate in the proximal tubule. It also directly promotes the reabsorption of calcium mainly in the distal tubule. A third action is the stimulation of 1,25 hydroxyvitamin D production in the proximal tubule. Conversely the hydroxyvitamin suppresses PTH secretion (negative feedback).

In bone, PTH acts on the osteoclast via the osteoblast. All the actions of the hormone on bone and the kidney are cyclic AMP dependent. It is only at supra-physiological concentrations that the resorptive effects of PTH on bone are observed.

111. Atrial receptors   Answer: C

The atria may play a crucial role in the control of body fluids. Free nerve endings are found throughout both the left and right atria. These project through myelinated and non-myelinated fibres in the vagii.

The efferent arc of the reflex is via the sympathetic cardiac nerves. Changes in renal blood flow and function occur, which may be mediated through the sympathetic system, but responses are also observed in demyelinated kidneys.

Stimulating atrial receptors produce an increase in water excretion and natriuresis within 5–10 minutes. A reduction in ADH, renin and aldosterone plasma levels is found.

Peptides are secreted by the atria – the major one is atrial natriuretic peptide. This inhibits sodium reabsorption in the distal nephron, promotes excretion of sodium and water (but not potassium) and antagonises the effects of noradrenaline and angiotensin II – particularly vasoconstriction.

112. Fat absorption and metabolism   Answers: CD

Chylomicrons are composed of triglycerides (90%), cholesterol, phospholipid and protein. They enter the blood stream from the lymph via the thoracic duct. Triglycerides are then removed by the peripheral cells through lipolysis (lipoprotein lipase). The small cholesterol rich chylomicron remnants are principally cleared by the liver by binding to receptors which recognise apolipoprotein E.

The liver secretes very low density lipoproteins (LDL) which are triglyceride rich. By the same process as above the triglycerides are removed leaving cholesterol rich LDL. It is LDL that is the principal delivery system of cholesterol. Peripheral cells bind the LDLs through receptors which recognise apolipoprotein B, their major protein component.

Cholesterol synthesis within the cells is inhibited by an abundance of LDL. The receptor synthesis is suppressed when cholesterol is not required (down regulation).

When very high levels of LDL are present the cholesterol can enter the cell by a non-receptor mediated route, which is important in atheroma formation.

113. Potassium homeostasis   Answer: D

The total body potassium in the adult male is approximately 3500 mmol of which 3000 mmol are exchangable. Only 50–60 mmol exist in the extracellular space. This state is maintained by the Gibbs–Donnan equilibrium with active transport of sodium requiring energy expenditure.

The normal dietary intake is 60–200 mmol/day. If the diet is potassium free then the kidney still excretes 10–20 mmol of the cation per litre of urine (cf. sodium). 85% of the filtered potassium is reabsorbed in the proximal tubule, most of the urine potassium is derived from distal tubule secretion. Here the urinary sodium is exchanged for both potassium and hydrogen ions, hence the relationship of potassium homoeostasis to acid–base disturbances. A fall in plasma pH of 0.1 causes a rise in serum potassium of approximately 1 mmol/l. Occasionally in severe exercise the levels may rise by as much as 2 mmol/l.

In the gastrointestinal tract potassium is absorbed in the proximal small bowel (passive) and secreted, in exchange for sodium, in the colon. Fluid lost from a gastric aspirate or upper intestinal fistula contains 10–15 mmol/l of potassium.

In diabetic ketoacidosis, even if the serum potassium is high, there is often a severe total body deficit. If both acidotic and hypokalaemic then giving bicarbonate to correct the former, together with insulin, will drive potassium back into the cells, which can induce life-threatening hypokalaemia.

114. The anion gap   Answers: ACDE

The anion gap is calculated from the formula:

$$\text{Anion gap} = Na^+ - (HCO_3^- + Cl^-)$$

Potassium is not used in the equation since it is relatively stable and contributes very little. The normal value is 12 ± 2 mEq/l. It is due to unmeasured anions (protein, phosphate, sulphate and other endogenous anions).

An elevated gap is virtually pathognomonic of a metabolic acidosis. A small 2-3 mEq/l rise is occasionally seen in respiratory and metabolic alkalosis.

The main endogenous aetiologies of an elevated gap are uraemia, lactic acidosis and diabetic ketoacidosis. The ingestion of salicylates, methanol, ethylene glycol and paraldehyde all produce a widening of the gap. The use of antibiotics with a high sodium content (e.g. carbenicillin) may also cause an increased level due to the unmeasured free drug.

If a patient is losing bicarbonate (from the kidney or GI tract) then the loss of bicarbonate is matched by an elevation of the serum chloride. The gap remains unchanged, but hyperchloraemic acidosis is found.

115. Water balance   Answer: E

60% of the total body weight (TBW) in males and 55% in females is composed of water. The difference is due to the higher fat content in females. One-third of the TBW is extracellular fluid.

The osmolarity of a solute is defined as the number of osmoles of solute per kilogram of solvent. It may be calculated from: $2(Na^+ + K^+) + $ urea $+$ glucose (in mmol/l). The normal range is 280–295 mOsmol/kg.

The normal osmolarity is monitored through osmoreceptors in the hypothalamus which can detect a 1% change in osmolarity (350 ml in a 70 kg man). ADH (Arginine vasopressin AVP) is secreted as a result from the posterior pituitary, being synthesised as a nonapeptide in the supra-optic and paraventricular nuclei in the hypothalamus. It acts on the distal renal tubule and collecting duct increasing resorption of water. Below 280 mOsmol/kg, ADH is undetectable, above 295 mOsmol/kg it is maximally secreted. The range of urine osmolality produced is 30-1200 mOsmol/kg. The kidneys have an obligate urine output of 0.5 l/24 h to excrete the osmotic load.

Colloid osmotic pressure is the osmotic effect due to the difference in concentration of large protein molecules in the capillaries and the extravascular fluid compartment. It is normally 20–25 mm Hg.

The average daily requirement for water is approximately 1500 ml.

116. Diabetes mellitus   Answers: ABC

Clinical features of a glucagonoma may include necrolytic migratory erythema, mild diabetes mellitus, psychiatric disturbances, diarrhoea and venous thrombosis.

Clinical features of a somatostatinoma may include dyspepsia, diabetes mellitus, gallstones, steatorrhoea and hypochlorhydria.

Cranial diabetes insipidus may be associated with diabetes mellitus, optic atrophy and deafness in the DIDMOAD (Wolfram's) syndrome.

Except in the very young child, in whom hypoglycaemia may occur, most individuals with growth hormone deficiency have a normal blood glucose concentration. Excess growth hormone (acromegaly) is associated with diabetes mellitus. The systemic effects of glucocorticoid deficiency (cf. Cushing's syndrome) include a tendency to develop spontaneous fasting hypoglycaemia not hyperglycaemia.

117. Hypothermia   Answers: BCE

There is evidence that elderly patients who develop hypothermia (core temperature less than 35°C or if severe less than 32°C) do so not only because of the low ambient temperature but also due to impaired thermoregulatory mechanisms. Precipitating factors, apart from immobility (strokes, falls etc.) include the administration of phenothiazines, diazepam, nitrazepam or morphine. Poisoning with alcohol or carbon monoxide should also be considered.

The effects are seen throughout the systems of the body. The skin is waxy and fat feels 'doughy'. Confusion, hallucinations, and psychotic features may appear. In the neurological system dysarthria, rigidity, ataxia and tremor are common. Both contraction and relaxation phases of the tendon jerks are prolonged (cf. myxoedema).

In the cardiovascular system rhythm disturbances range from sinus bradycardia through to ventricular fibrillation. Some degree of heart block occurs in most patients. On the ECG a tremor, J wave, prolonged QT and T wave inversion may all be found.

Hypopnoea is common with periodic respiration. PO_2 and PCO_2 are low (the latter due to reduced production); in the final stages the PCO_2 rises with the deepening depression of the respiratory drive.

Haemoglobin and packed cell volume rise, a leucocytosis is common and thrombocytopenia is often found. Disseminated intravascular coagulation can be precipitated. Plasma viscosity is raised (cryofibrinogen and perhaps cryoglobulin). An elevated blood sugar is seen. Tests of thyroid function are unreliable until the patient is rewarmed. Hyponatraemia, raised creatinine kinase and hyperamylasaemia may be found.

NEPHROLOGY

118. Proximal tubule system   Answers: CDE

The proximal tubule system (PTS) consists of the early (S1) and late (S2) parts of the convoluted tubule and the medullary section of the proximal tubule (S3).

About 60% of glomerular ultrafiltrate is resorbed in the PTS while a constant Na^+ concentration is maintained along its length. Na^+ resorbtion is mainly energy dependent.

Amino acids, sugars, and organic and inorganic ions are actively resorbed, particularly in S1.

A variety of organic anions (including urate), cations and drugs are actively secreted, particularly in S2.

The combined actions of the thin limbs of the loop of Henlé and the collecting ducts determine final urine concentration (or dilution).

The majority of filtered bicarbonate is resorbed in the PTS but the distal nephron determines the net acid excretion which is normally equal to 1mEq/kg body weight/day.

119. Renal artery stenosis   Answers: ABD

Atheromatous renal artery stenoses are predominantly found in middle-aged and elderly males and tend to be proximally situated.

Fibromuscular hyperplasia, which may be unilateral or bilateral, is predominantly found in younger females and is more distally situated.

Intravenous pyelography characteristically reveals a small kidney on the affected side with a delayed and persistent nephrogram.

An abdominal bruit is uncommon.

A variety of surgical techniques are used to treat this condition, including autotransplantation to the iliac fossa. Long-term prognosis is better in the fibromuscular hyperplasia group, since in the atheromatous group, disease is often widespread throughout the arterial tree.

120. Membranous nephropathy   Answers: ABCE

This usually develops in the absence of any identifiable aetiological agent (i.e. it is 'idiopathic'), but recognised causal associations include infections (e.g. hepatitis), malignancy, drugs and systemic diseases (e.g. SLE). It occurs more frequently in HLA DR3 individuals in Caucasian populations.

Most patients present with a nephrotic syndrome, some with asymptomatic proteinuria. Macroscopic haematuria is rare.

Uniform thickening of the glomerular basement membrane (GBM) on light microscopy, 'beaded' deposition of IgG and C3 on immunofluorescence and discrete electron dense deposits along the subepithelial border of the GBM on electron microscopy are the pathological hallmarks.

Males are twice as commonly affected as females.

About 25% of patients will develop end stage renal failure. The prognosis is worse for adult males with heavy persisting proteinuria, hypertension and impaired renal function at presentation.

121. Minimal change nephropathy   Answers: CD

Minimal change nephropathy (MCN) is predominantly a disease of young males; 90% of childhood nephrotic syndrome is due to MCN, but only 10–20% in adults.

The only histological abnormality is retraction of the foot process on electron microscopy.

Proteinuria is usually heavy, but 'selective', and remits promptly with corticosteroid therapy. Cyclophosphamide may be used in patients who relapse frequently.

Despite a sometimes relapsing course, the prognosis should be excellent in patients who are appropriately treated.

Alport's syndrome is transmitted as an autosomal dominant condition but males are more severely affected. It is characterised by nerve deafness, cataracts, defects of the cornea and lens (sometimes), and a characteristic glomerulonephritis. The complete triad may not be present, but when severely affected the patients will die from renal failure before the age of 40 years.

122. Cystinuria   Answers: AD

Cystinuria is an autosomal recessive condition with a number of variants resulting in failure of cystine transport across gut and renal tubule cells because of abnormalities in specific transport mechanisms.

It is usually accompanied by failure to resorb lysine, arginine and ornithine, which also appear in the urine and can be detected by amino acid chromatography.

Stones develop when the solubility (300 mg/l) is exceeded. Stone formation is aggravated by acidic urine and they are faintly opaque due to the presence of sulphur and some calcium. There are frequently large staghorn calculi, which may lead to obstruction, infection and renal failure.

There are no associated dysmorphic abnormalities.

Treatment consists of: prevention (and sometimes dissolution) by a high fluid intake (more than 4 litres, spread over 24 hours); penicillamine, which binds cystine and prevents its crystallisation; and alkalinisation of the urine. Surgery and lithotripsy may be indicated.

123. Renal changes during pregnancy   Answers: ABDE

Renal blood flow and glomerular filtration rate increase dramatically in early pregnancy and are sustained.

Kidney (and glomerular) size increase and there is often dilatation of the collecting systems. Acute pyelonephritis is prevented by appropriate antibiotics for asymptomatic bacteriuria. Hypertension may be discovered for the first time in pregnancy, may be only associated with the pregnancy (pre-eclampsia) or may be due to underlying conditions. In a normal pregnancy, diastolic blood pressure falls.

124. Normal human kidney   Answers: BCE

Each kidney weighs about 150 g and contains 1 million or more glomeruli.

20% of the resting cardiac output goes to the kidneys (more than 1 litre per minute) of which 90% or more is directed to the cortex.

Total glomerular filtration is about 180 litres/day of which about 99% is resorbed in the tubules leaving an average urine output, depending on fluid intake, of 1–2 litres/day.

Production of renin, erythropoietin, 1,25 dihydroxycholecalciferol takes place in renal tissue.

125. Acute renal failure   Answers: ACE

Acute renal failure (ARF) is best considered as:

- Pre-renal i.e. effective volume depletion
- Intrinsic
- Post-renal i.e. obstructive.

Intrinsic ARF is most commonly due to either ischaemic or nephrotoxic acute tubular necrosis (ATN), but may also be due to interstitial nephritis, glomerulonephritis etc.

Absolute anuria is rare except in obstruction, bilateral renal artery occlusion, cortical necrosis or occasionally glomerulonephritis.

Kidney size may be normal or increased in acute obstruction or ATN. In an acute on chronic disease, renal size and anatomy may reflect the underlying condition.

The following features indicate pre-renal failure rather than established ATN:

- Urine : Plasma (U/P) osmolality greater than 1.5
- U/P creatinine greater than 40
- U/P urea ratio greater than 10
- Urinary sodium less than 20 mmol/l.

Treatment is aimed at the underlying condition and may be sufficient to prevent dialysis, or the condition may be rapidly self-limiting. Dialysis is indicated for fluid overload, hyperkalaemia, severe acidosis, uraemia, or a progressive rise in serum creatinine especially if rapid.

126. Chronic renal failure (CRF)   Answers: BCD

Phosphate retention in CRF is usually treated by giving aluminium hydroxide orally with meals to bind phosphate in the gut and prevent absorption. Calcium carbonate, with food, has a similar effect.

Acute (and also acute on chronic) renal failure is occasionally precipitated by the use of contrast media for urography, angiography and cholecystography. Any impairment is usually mild and transient, but even this may be significant if the glomerulas filtration rate (GFR) is already markedly reduced. It is more common in elderly people, in diabetes, in myeloma and with dehydration.

Nocturia is associated with inflammatory disease of the lower urinary tract. It is also associated with loss of concentrating ability in CRF.

Low protein diets were originally used in CRF to prevent the accumulation of 'uraemic toxins' and to improve uraemic symptoms before the widespread availability of dialysis. We now know that low protein diets (around 0.5 g/kg body weight) introduced early in the course of renal failure may slow the rate of decline of GFR. In diabetics, the use of ACE inhibitors slows progression of renal disease.

Despite the hyperuricaemia which accompanies CRF, for an unexplained reason, clinical gout is rare and prophylactic treatment is not indicated.

127. Disordered mineral metabolism   Answers: ABCDE

The skeletal abnormalities associated with CRF (renal osteodystrophy) include hyperparathyroidism, osteomalacia, osteoporosis, periosteal new bone formation and osteonecrosis. Soft tissue calcification occurs especially in blood vessels, around joints and in the conjunctiva (band keratopathy).

Resorption of the terminal phalanges causes pseudoclubbing. Subperiosteal bone resorption is particularly marked along the radial border of the middle phalanges and the outer ends of the clavicles.

Radiographic features of osteomalacia, e.g. Looser's zones are best seen in the pelvic bones. In children, radiographic changes simulate rickets. The horizontal banding pattern of reduced bone density interposed with sclerosis in the vertebrae is referred to as 'rugger-jersey' spine.

Fracturing osteodystrophy is associated with osteomalacia in combination with aluminium toxicity.

Biochemical changes of renal osteodystrophy include raised parathormone levels, increased serum bone alkaline phosphatase (in renal tubular disorders alkaline phosphatase can be low or normal), low serum calcium (unless tertiary hyperparathyroidism supervenes) and high serum phosphate.

128. Adult polycystic kidney disease — Answers: ABDE

Adult polycystic kidney disease (APCKD) is an autosomal dominant inherited disease, the mutant gene being found on the short arm of chromosome 16. 85% of families carry the same gene – PKD1.

Cysts which increase in size with age, are found in both kidneys and may also be present in the liver, pancreas, spleen and lungs. Berry aneurysms may be found on the circle of Willis.

Malignancy developing within the cyst is a rare but recognised complication. The condition usually presents with abdominal discomfort or haematuria, occasionally with renal colic or with features either of chronic renal failure or hypertension.

Affected people are frequently unable to retain salt appropriately and therefore become volume depleted. They usually maintain their haemoglobin despite severe renal failure (erythropoietin production continues).

129. Urinary tract infection — Answers: ABC

Urinary tract infection (UTI) is common in normal adult females. It is uncommon in men and children unless there is an underlying abnormality and always requires further investigation.

There is an increased incidence of UTI associated with the older age groups. UTI is also associated with obstruction e.g. enlarged prostate, stricture formation and urethral valves, with stone formation (therefore medullary sponge kidney), with residual urine e.g. cystocoele and with instrumentation.

Pathogenic *E. coli* have an increased ability to attach to epithelial cells via their fimbriae. It is the commonest organism in uncomplicated UTI. Infection responds to a single oral dose of antibiotic in 80% of cases.

A sterile pyuria suggests TB, calculi, fastidious organism, analgesic nephropathy or a partially treated infection.

The cause of loss of concentrating ability in UTI is poorly understood. Note the *not* in part E, this frequently causes problems for candidates who fail to read it.

130. Renal transplantation   Answers: BCE

There are few absolute contraindications to transplantation and it is now being performed at the extremes of age down to 2 years and over 65 years. It is rarely performed for patients with oxalosis or bronchiectasis (amyloidosis), but SLE only very occasionally recurs in the graft.

Malignancy, especially of skin, lymphoma and reticulum cell sarcoma have an increased incidence in the transplant population.

There is an increased risk of many types of infection in transplant patients that may be missed in the early stages due to the effects of immunosuppression. Viral infection, notably cytomegalovirus and herpes zoster are common. Unusual infections e.g. candida (especially oral and oesophageal) and pneumocystis occur with an increased frequency.

ABO incompatability is an absolute contraindication to transplantation. In cadaveric grafting, different centres use different criteria as to the acceptability of various degrees of HLA matching that is required. The most important antigens appear to be those of the HLA B and DR series.

Graft survival (at one year) between identical twins should exceed 90%. In cadaveric grafting the 70% plus graft survival with 'conventional' immunosuppression (prednisolone and azathioprine) is increased to 85–90% using cyclosporin A.

131. Obstructive uropathy   Answers: ABCD

Obstruction of the urinary tract, as with any tube, may be intraluminal, intramural or due to extramural compression. Calculi, blood clot, stricture, tumour, prostatic enlargement, neurogenic bladder and pelvi-ureteric junction obstruction are the commonest causes. Retroperitoneal fibrosis, either idiopathic or associated with prolonged methysergide therapy may be responsible.

Urethral (e.g. postgonococcal or traumatic) and ureteral (e.g. TB or post-calculi) strictures must be considered.

Prolonged partial obstruction will result in loss of concentrating ability and polyuria. A marked postobstructive diuresis is also recognised and, if uncorrected, may lead to severe volume depletion and electrolyte imbalance.

Impaired glomerular filtration rate (GFR) may be fully reversible even after prolonged complete obstruction. Occasionally it may lead to end stage renal failure even if the obstruction is relieved.

132. Urine discolouration   Answers: ADE

You should try and categorise abnormalities of urine colour. A useful scheme is: Drugs e.g. levodopa (brown) or rifampicin (red) or dyes e.g. beetroot (pink-red).

Rhabdomyolysis (myoglobinuria) or acute intravascular haemolysis (haemoglobinuria) can colour the urine red.

The urine may darken upon standing in several conditions including acute porphyria and alkaptonuria.

133. Renal acidosis   Answer: B

Renal tubular acidosis (RTA) can be divided into:

- Type I – distal RTA with hypokalaemia, causes include sickle cell anaemia, and chronic active liver disease
- Type II – proximal RTA, causes include myeloma and Sjögrens syndrome
- Type III – very rare and has manifestations of both Type I and Type II
- Type IV – distal with hyperkalaemia

The underlying defect in Type IV RTA is either deficiency or reduced action of aldosterone. This may be due to reduced renin levels as in diabetic nephropathy, tubulointerstitial diseases such as chronic atrophic pyelonephritis or patients on NSAIDs. Alternatively, Addison's disease or, less commonly, inborn errors of aldosterone synthesis may be responsible.

Patients have hyperkalaemia and a normal anion gap acidosis (i.e. raised chloride and reduced bicarbonate). There may be moderate renal impairment, but the hyperkalaemia is out of proportion to the reduction in GFR.

There is no evidence of any significant defect in proximal tubular function (i.e. reabsorption of bicarbonate, amino acids, glucose).

Patients may be treated with fludrocortisone and possibly bicarbonate.

GASTROENTEROLOGY

134. Crohn's disease   Answers: BD

The peak incidence of Crohn's disease is between the ages of 15 and 35 years, but there is a second peak in older people. Hence, it is increasing in prevalence due to the rising number of elderly people in the population, but overall the incidence does not appear to be rising.

The terminal ileum is still the most common site of disease, but in elderly individuals, distal colonic colitis accounts for nearly half of all the cases. If the distal colon is involved, perianal problems are often found. The disease can appear anywhere along the GI tract. In elderly people, the disease often remains isolated to one segment and carries a better prognosis.

Diverticular disease increases in incidence with increasing age, the commonest site being the sigmoid colon. It often presents with altered bowel habit, pain or tenesmus. Complications include sepsis with severe systemic disturbance, frank haemorrhage or anaemia, and fistula formation. Differentiation from Crohn's disease is often difficult and requires multiple biopsies under direct vision.

135. Colonic pseudo-obstruction   Answers: BD

The highest incidence is in elderly individuals, but it can appear at any age. Often it occurs in patients already confined to hospital for some other reason, e.g. fractured hip or pelvis leading to immobility (which decreases bowel transit time). Predisposing factors are electrolyte disturbance, anaemia or dehydration.

The symptoms are identical to colonic obstruction with gradual abdominal distension and high pitched bowel sounds.

Plain radiographs are compatible, but often not typical of large bowel obstruction with gaseous distension. Contrast radiology or direct visualisation with the sigmoidoscope or colonoscope can be used to assess whether obstruction is present.

The management is conservative with correction of electrolyte and fluid abnormalities; decompression can be achieved with a flatus tube. Mortality is higher after surgery and this should be reserved for those patients with impending perforation.

136. Drug-induced gastrointestinal ulceration   Answers: ABD

There is a clear association between gastrointestinal ulceration, haemorrhage and perforation, and the ingestion of non-steroidal anti-inflammatory drugs. Elderly people are particularly at risk from these complications. Ibuprofen appears to be associated with less risk, but this is probably due to lower dose. Enteric coated and rectal preparations of NSAIDs are still associated with gastric damage.

Doxycycline can cause oesophageal ulceration unless swallowed with plenty of water. Tablets or capsules taken with only small amounts of water immediately prior to retiring for the night can lead to oesophageal ulceration and stenosis. Ascorbic acid can also cause oesophageal ulceration.

Tripotassium dicitratobismuthate (TDB) is DeNol, used in the treatment of peptic ulceration. The rate of relapse after the cessation of therapy is less than that after cimetidine or ranitidine.

Spironolactone has been linked with peptic ulceration, indomethacin with small bowel ulceration. Slow K is contraindicated in the presence of GI obstruction or stasis because of local irritant effects.

137. Acute proctitis   Answers: ABCDE

The differential diagnosis of an ulcerative proctitis requires direct visualisation, biopsies, swabs for microbiology including virology, and radiological studies.

Infective causes include:

- Gonnorrhoea with stinging rectal pain and pus
- Bacillary dysentery especially shigellosis
- Amoebiasis – history of travel, discrete ulcers, swabs showing motile trophozoites
- Herpes simplex colitis notably in homosexuals and those with the acquired immune deficiency syndrome

Lymphogranuloma venereum is a sexually transmitted infection with *Chlamydia trachomatis*. Anal intercourse can lead to a haemorrhagic proctocolitis with regional lymphadenitis. Acute infections have non-specific features (fever, leucocytosis), a transient primary genital lesion followed by multi locular suppurative regional lymphadenopathy. Rarely systemic complications can occur such as meningoencephalitis. After a latent period of years, genital elephantiasis, strictures, and fistulae of the urethra, penis and rectum may develop. Treatment is with tetracycline, erythromycin or a sulphonamide.

Ischaemic proctitis is rare due to good collateral vascular supply via the iliac arteries. More important differential diagnoses are ulcerative colitis (where the rectum is always involved) and Crohn's disease.

Other rare causes include radiation and Behçet's syndrome.

138. Investigation of malabsorption   Answers: BCE

The commonest causes of malabsorption are mucosal diseases (e.g. coeliac) where changes on radiology are non-specific. Radiology should be reserved for patients with suspected anatomical abnormalities.

Biopsies from the second part of the duodenum taken at endoscopy, if normal, exclude coeliac disease. Small bowel biopsy may be diagnostic in Whipple's disease (PAS positive glycoproteins), abetalipoproteinaemia (cells vacuolated due to excess fat), and agammaglobulinaemia (flattened villi, increased lymphocyte infiltration, absence of plasma cells). It may also be useful in the diagnosis of lymphoma, lymphangiectasia, amyloidosis and parasitic infections.

Samples of jejunal juice may be helpful in giardiasis and bacterial overgrowth. Giardiasis is an infestation with the protozoa *Giardia lamblia*. It is more common in children, though previous gastrectomy is a predisposing factor in adults. Mostly the infection is asymptomatic but nausea, flatulence, pain, distension and watery diarrhoea occurs. Treatment is with metronidazole.

The terminal ileum is visualised in 70% of patients at barium enema. The Schilling test, with and without intrinsic factor, is a useful test of function.

The investigation of chronic pancreatitis is difficult. In 50% calcification is seen on a plain radiograph or image intensifier. Ultrasound and CT studies may be abnormal, ERCP is a very useful diagnostic investigation.

139. Diarrhoea in AIDS   Answers: ABCE

Any unusual organism isolated from the rectum should alert the clinician to the diagnosis, but gonococcus, lymphogranuloma venereum, herpes simplex, *Giardia lamblia* and cytomegalovirus may be found.

A full range of investigations is required for accurate diagnosis. In particular, cytomegalovirus may only be diagnosed by histological examination.

Whilst all bodily fluids from AIDS patients should be treated with caution, HIV has not been isolated from stools. However, beware bloody diarrhoea. There have been only a small number of proven cases of seroconversion from any source in health workers caring for infected patients.

Cryptosporidium can cause a severe diarrhoea which is often recurrent. It is often difficult to treat but may respond to erythromycin.

140. *Campylobacter and Helicobacter*   Answers: ABCD

Campylobacter jejuni is a thermophylic vibrio-like organism, which is a major cause of gastroenteritis. The typical illness is an enterocolitis accompanied by a low grade fever, systemic upset, profuse diarrhoea and severe abdominal pain occasionally mimicking acute appendicitis.

It is usually self-limiting but bloody diarrhoea occurs and symptoms may be prolonged. Barium enema may show typical ulcerative colitis-like features. Septicaemia and post-infective arthropathy are rare complications. No specific treatment is indicated for the acute attacks but oral erythromycin may be useful if severe, and gentamycin in septicaemia.

Campylobacter jejuni is a common zoonosis with carriage being endemic in farm and domestic animals.

141. Liver biopsy   Answers: ABCE

In a good risk patient a percutaneous liver biopsy is usually an uncomplicated procedure, following which the patient can go home after a few hours rest. The patient must be able to control his respiration to prevent capsular tear. Higher risk is encountered in jaundiced patients (vitamin K_1 10 mg for 2 days) and should not be performed if the prothrombin time is prolonged more than 3 s over the control unless under cover of fresh frozen plasma. The platelet count should be >80,000. The patient's blood group should be known.

In a review of 20,000 cases mortality was 0.17%. Haemorrhage occurs in

0.5%, but is the commonest significant complication. It is very rare in patients who are not jaundiced. Biliary peritonitis is more common in bile duct (extrahepatic) obstruction or cholestasis. It rarely requires surgical intervention. Biopsy (percutaneous) is often performed under ultrasound guidance, particularly if the abnormality is localised or patchy. Bacteraemia occurs in about 15% of patients during liver biopsy, the organisms are usually Gram-negative. Occasionally septic shock may develop.

In the presence of ascites, a cirrhotic liver (small and fibrous) is difficult to puncture and capsular lacerations can occur. Difficulties may also be encountered in patients with pulmonary emphysema. Biopsy is absolutely contraindicated in haemangiomas of the liver.

142. Fatty infiltration of the liver   Answers: BCDE

Fatty infiltration of the liver occurs in many diverse conditions (e.g. alcoholism, diabetes mellitus, kwashiorkor, pregnancy, Wilson's disease, tuberculosis, inflammatory bowel disease and cystic fibrosis). The spleen may be enlarged if there is portal hypertension, but there is no associated fatty infiltration.

The distribution of the fatty infiltration depends on the aetiology and associated metabolic derangement. It may be segmented, lobar or 'spotty'.

Fat is bright on ultrasound and of low density on CT. Diagnosis is highly reliable in the correct clinical setting, particularly if both ultrasound and CT are typically abnormal.

It can occur in any chronically debilitated patient (e.g. kwashiorkor, alcoholism) including those in need of total parenteral nutrition.

In chronic alcoholism, fatty change is commonly found and disappears with abstinence and good diet. However, the return to histological normality depends on the degree of fibrosis from prolonged hepatic damage. Fatty liver is probably of little importance to the development of cirrhosis.

143. Bile acid diarrhoea   Answers: ABCD

Bile acids are synthesised only in the liver, 0.3–0.7 g being produced and lost in the faeces each day. Cholic acid and chenodeoxycholic acid (primary bile acids) are produced from cholesterol. When these come into contact with bacteria in the small bowel (overgrowth) or colon 7- deoxycholic and lithocholic acids are produced. Bile acids are conjugated in the liver with glycine or taurine to form bile salts. These are actively excreted against an enormous gradient into bile. The salts then enter into a micelle formation with cholesterol and phospholipids. They are reabsorbed only in the terminal ileum. Failure to do so causes excess amounts to reach the colon where the salts are highly irritant and produced diarrhoea. Causes include surgery or Crohn's disease.

Cholestyramine binds bile salts in the intestine and the complexes are eliminated in the faeces. It lowers serum bile salt and cholesterol levels (xanthomas in cholestasis diminish). Faecal fat excretion can also interfere with absorption of the fat soluble vitamins (A,D,E,K).

The formation of gallstones is dependent on the relative composition of bile salt micelles. Hence, if bile salt loss occurs, relative bile cholesterol concentration is altered and the saturation index favours stone deposition.

144. Hepatic adenoma   Answers: BE

Cavernous or capillary haemangiomata are the most common benign liver lesions, being found in up to 5% of autopsies. They are usually asymptomatic, situated peripherally in the posterior subcapsular part of the right lobe of the liver and are discovered incidentally on ultrasound examination. Occasionally a vascular hum may be heard, and rarely the tumour may rupture.

There is an unequivocal association between hepatic adenoma, a very rare tumour, and contraceptive use. Prolonged use increases the risk, which has been estimated at 3–4 per 100,000 users. There is also an association between adenoma formation and the C17 substituted testosterones (along with peliosis, hepatocellular carcinoma and angiosarcoma).

Hepatic adenomas are usually single, but in about 5% may be multiple. Usually, they are asymptomatic, but may present with a mass, haemorrhage or tumour infarction. Treatment is initially conservative with stopping any associated sex hormone. Rupture is more likely in pregnancy. Surgery is reserved for complications.

Ultrasound can be useful as can CT scans. However, both can fail to demonstrate the tumour when it closely resembles normal liver. Arteriography shows stretching of the feeding arteries around the mass.

145. Medical therapy for duodenal ulcer   Answers: ACDE

Studies have shown no difference in healing rates with ranitidine or cimetidine using single or divided daily doses. Cimetidine has been associated with more side-effects notably diarrhoea, confusion in elderly people, myalgia and rarely interstitial nephritis or pancreatitis. The dose should be reduced in renal failure. It can also prolong the elimination of drugs removed by oxidation in the liver. Of clinical importance are the interactions with warfarin, theophylline and phenytoin.

Bismuth-containing compounds (e.g. DeNol) have lower recurrence rates up to twelve months after healing compared with H_2 blockers.

Failure to heal is often due to poor compliance. H_2 blockers should heal a duoderal ulcer even if associated with the Zollinger-Ellison syndrome (non-beta cell tumour i.e a gastrinoma that in 10% of cases is found outside the pancreas).

You should be aware of the link between *Helicobacter pylori* and gastroduodenal disease, not simply because of understanding the basic mechanisms, but choice of therapy. Many people are infected with *H. pylori* and more than half the population over the age of 50 have evidence of gastritis. However, in the absence of peptic ulceration, you should not try to eradicate the organism.

Antimicrobial therapy may be used in peptic ulceration. Currently, many units do not routinely culture for *H. pylori* in patients presenting for the first time, but do so when the ulcer fails to heal or recurs. There are also diagnostic serum antibody tests available. The approach is a combination of a specific anti-ulcer drug together with one or more antimicrobials. A reasonable approach is triple therapy with bismuth, metronidazole and tetracycline. Alternatively, a combination of omeprazole and amoxycillin may be used.

146. Upper gastrointestinal haemorrhage   Answers: BC

A Mallory–Weis tear (60% below gastro-oesophageal junction, remainder involve the junction or oesophagus) can occur in up to 20% in some series. The rates quoted are dependent on the timing of the investigations, most tears heal very quickly and rarely rebleed.

Bleeding may cease with hypotension and hypovolaemia and restart with resuscitation. Old patients tolerate further bleeding poorly (remember association with NSAIDs) because of concomitant cardiac disease etc. and should be operated on early.

A visible vessel in an ulcer base or fresh clot in an ulcer is associated with about 50% risk of rebleed. A posterior duodenal ulcer may erode into the gastroduodenal artery with catastrophic consequences. Due to erosion into the pancreas pain may be felt in the back. There have been no differences reported in the rates of rebleeding of peptic ulcers in different sites.

147. Oesophageal varices
Answers: AE

In the management of acutely bleeding varices there are several options. The Sengstaken–Blakemore tube can be used, but if left for longer than 24 hours ulceration can occur. Other complications include asphyxia and obstruction of the pharynx. Tubes are now rarely required. Somatostatin is highly effective and appears to have fewer systemic side-effects than Glypressin (triglycyl lysine vasopressin). The half-life of somatostatin is 6–12 hours. Side-effects include hypertension, coronary artery spasm, facial pallor, abdominal colic and evacuation of the bowel.

The size of varix is not necessarily related to portal pressure and does not appear to be a good predictor of the risk of bleeding. The reason why varices bleed is unclear. However oesophageal varices are more likely to bleed than gastric varices, possibly because of local factors such as oesophagitis or vomiting.

Endoscopic sclerotherapy reduces the risk of recurrent bleeding and has had a major impact in reducing episodes. Following sclerosis, varices do recur in most patients, often in more inaccessible places, e.g. fundus of the stomach. Propranolol reduces portal pressure and is used prophylactically to prevent bleeding.

148. Ultrasound examination of the biliary system
Answers: ABCDE

Oral cholecystography and biliary ultrasound are similar in terms of specificity and sensitivity. Ultrasound can detect stones of 3 mm and greater with a specificity of 97% and a moderate sensitivity of 88%.

The cause of bile duct obstruction can be demonstrated in the majority of cases. However in about 5% of obstructive jaundice the bile ducts are not dilated at the time of examination, especially if the jaundice is not severe or is of short duration.

Ultrasound can also be used for examination of the portal vein (especially important in patients with varices, to determine whether the vein is patent). Space-occupying lesions of the liver of about 2 cm in diameter and occasionally 1 cm can be visualised. Metastases, primary liver cancer, cysts or abscesses can be identified. Ultrasonography also demonstrates ascites.

149. Halothane hepatotoxicity

Answers: ADE

There is very good evidence that halothane is hepatotoxic with an incidence of 1 in 10-35000 anaesthetics producing a serious hepatitis. It increases in frequency with the number of exposures and short time between them. However, it can occur after a single exposure and about 30% of patients who develop fulminant liver failure after the first anaesthetic will die. Mortality rises to about 40% after two and 50% after three exposures.

The aetiology of the liver damage is not clear but hypoxia has no proven role.

The most common cause of fulminant liver failure is hepatitis due to A, B or C virus. Drug reactions are the next group with paracetamol, isoniazid, phenelzine and halothane predominating. In any post-anaesthetic patient, viral hepatitis can be difficult to exclude. The prognosis is dependent on the grade of coma reached, but in those with rapidly progressing failure a successful transplant may be the only option.

150. Enteral feeding

Answers: BCDE

Enteral feeding is widely used in a variety of conditions because of the availability of PEG tubes. Complications include nausea, vomiting, diarrhoea, hyperglycaemia, aspiration and peritonitis

Diarrhoea, nausea and abdominal pain can be minimised by constant infusion of feed rather than by giving boluses. It is the osmotic load (osmoles/unit time) that is of importance rather than the osmoles/unit volume. Diluted 'starter' regimes are often not required.

Patients who require feeding for more than 4 weeks will need supplementary vitamins and trace elements. The feeds are gluten and lactulose free.

The most important factor is the non-nitrogen/calorie:nitrogen ratio. A ratio of 150–200:1 is suitable for most non-catabolic patients together with a calorie intake of 30–35 cal/kg. In hypercatabolic states the ratio reduces to

120–150:1 with a calorie requirement of 40–45 kcal/kg. A low sodium feed can be used if the patient is in danger of sodium overload.

HAEMATOLOGY

151. Disseminated intravascular coagulation (DIC)   Answers: BC

Thrombocytopenia is found in the majority of cases of DIC due to platelet consumption in peripheral microthrombi. A persistently normal platelet count makes the diagnosis of DIC unlikely.

Due to the relatively short half-lives of factors V and VIII in the circulation it is these two factors in particular that are rapidly consumed and result in the abnormal coagulation tests.

FDPs are almost always elevated (although occasionally they may be normal in cases of chronic DIC, e.g. associated with malignancy). FDPs have an anticoagulant action as they inhibit thrombin, fibrin polymerisation, thromboplastin generation and platelet function.

152. Paroxysmal nocturnal haemoglobinuria (PNH)   Answers: ABCDE

The underlying abnormality that affects red blood cells, granulocytes and platelets in PNH is sensitivity to complement. Antibody is not always necessary for complement fixation, C3 is readily attached by means of the alternative pathway.

Pancytopenia is a common form of presentation of PNH and this should be excluded in all cases of idiopathic aplastic anaemia. Although progression of PNH to acute leukaemia is uncommon it is nevertheless a well recognised complication (together with the myelodysplastic syndromes).

Most patients with PNH and longstanding haemoglobinuria show reduced renal function due to pyelonephritis, renal papillary necrosis and chronic renal failure. Iron deficiency is common due to chronic intravascular haemolysis and iron loss in the urine.

Patients with PNH are prone to both arterial and venous thrombosis, which can present as intracranial or intra-abdominal occlusions such as hepatic venous thrombosis (Budd–Chiari syndrome).

153. Secondary erythrocytosis   Answers: ABCE

Polycythaemia may be divided into primary, as in polycythaemia rubra vera in which all the cell lines may be affected, and secondary where there is red cell overproduction (secondary erythrocytosis) as a response to a stimulus.

The investigation of choice is estimation of red cell mass and plasma volume. Differentiation can be made between absolute polycythaemia and relative (dehydration) or pseudo (Gaisböck's syndrome) polycythaemia in which the red cell mass is normal and plasma volume is reduced – associated with hypertension and diuretics.

Hydronephrosis is associated with increased red cell production as are many other benign and malignant renal conditions. In carboxyhaemoglobinaemia the shift to the left of the oxygen dissociation curve results in impaired oxygen delivery to the tissues and secondary erythrocytosis. Approximately 10% of patients with hepatoma may develop increased red cell mass due to production of erythropoietin-like material by the tumour. The exact cause of the association between uterine leiomyoma and polycythaemia is unknown.

154. Peripheral blood basophilia   Answers: ACD

Basophilia is frequently seen in the myeloproliferative disorders such as chronic myeloid leukaemia, myelofibrosis and polycythaemia rubra vera. Excessive basophilia may indicate the transformation of chronic myeloid leukaemia into an accelerated form or 'blastic' phase. Basophilia does not characteristically occur in secondary polycythaemia.

Chronic inflammatory bowel disease such as ulcerative colitis may be associated with basophilia.

Urticaria pigmentosa (brown macules/papules overlying clusters of mast cells, urticarial wheals when rubbed, may rarely develop into systemic mastocytosis) results in increased numbers of mast cells as opposed to basophils.

155. Henoch–Schönlein disease   Answers: CE

Henoch–Schönlein disease (purpura) is predominantly an acute vascular abnormality and the platelet count is normal. The vasculitic purpura is distributed over the lower part of the body particularly the buttocks. There is an association with colicky abdominal pain, gastrointestinal haemorrhage and kidney disease. It is more common in children, but occurs in adults.

The aetiology is unknown and the disease is self limiting (4–6 weeks) with the purpura occuring in crops. Occasionally the disease can persist for a few months. There is no treatment, steroids are ineffective.

Renal involvement occurs in approximately 40% with, in the majority, the only abnormality being microscopic haematuria. In severe cases a focal or diffuse glomerulonephritis may be found with IgA, C3 and fibrin deposits. Rarely the disease can progress to acute renal failure.

Hess's test (the appearance of purpura in the forearm with a sphygmomanometer cuff at 80–100 mm Hg for 5 minutes) is often positive but is of little diagnostic value.

156. Chronic lymphatic leukaemia (CLL)   Answers: BDE

In CLL immunoglobulin levels are usually reduced (immune paresis) and contribute towards recurrent infections. Paraproteins are sometimes present.

Thrombocytopenia and anaemia (unless associated with haemolysis) tend to occur in the more advanced states of the disease and are associated with a poorer prognosis.

Haemolytic anaemia in CLL is usually associated with a positive direct Coombs' test (other associations are drugs (e.g. methyldopa), SLE and lymphomay or other malignancy) and warm antibodies (usually IgG occasionally IgA), which may show specificity to the Rhesus blood group system.

As well as hypogammaglobulinaemia, mediastinal lymph gland enlargement may result in airway obstruction and recurrent chest infections which can be a considerable clinical problem. Unlike many other advanced malignancies, cellular immunity is usually preserved.

157. Haemophilia A   Answers: CDE

The severity of the bleeding diathesis in haemophilia A is very similar to that of haemophilia B (factor IX deficiency) and the conditions cannot be separated purely on the basis of clinical criteria.

The prothrombin time is a good screening test of the vitamin K coagulation factors (II, VII, IX, X, liver dependent) and is normal in haemophilia A. The partial thromboplastin time is prolonged in moderate and severe cases of haemophilia.

Factor IX concentrates may be of benefit in haemophilia A patients (who are factor VIII deficient) who have antibodies (inhibitors) against factor VIII.

The majority of haemophiliacs have a good life expectancy; cerebral haemorrhage is still a common cause of death. Up to 90% of patients have antibodies against the hepatitis B virus (HBsAb positive), although HBsAg positivity is uncommon. Chronic hepatitis is a problem because of transmission of hepatitis C virus. There is a cohort of haemophiliacs who developed AIDS because of exposure to infected blood products.

158. Von Willebrand's disease   Answers: DE

Von Willebrand's disease (VWD) is a hereditary haemorrhagic disease transmitted as an autosomal dominant trait. Consanguineous offspring may have the clinically more severe homozygous form of the disease. The diagnosis is based on the laboratory findings of a prolonged bleeding time (platelet and blood vessel abnormality), low factor VIII procoagulant activity and, unlike haemophilia, an approximately parallel reduction in factor VIII antigenic activity.

Although the bleeding time in VWD is usually prolonged, a normal bleeding time does not exclude the diagnosis. Blood vessels appear normal on light microscopy.

Haemarthroses are less common than in haemophilia although recurrent epistaxis and menorrhagia may present problems due to the associated platelet functional abnormality.

Transfusion of haemophiliac plasma to a VWD patient may raise the factor VIII level due to the transfer of a humoral factor (VW factor) deficient in VWD patients, but present in haemophiliacs.

159. Macrocytic non-megaloblastic anaemia   Answers: ABC

Various types of anaemia can occur in liver disease but abnormalities of lipid metabolism or alcoholic liver disease can result in macrocytosis. Hypothyroidism *per se* can result in macrocytosis. Aplastic anaemia, particularly the uncommon cases where spontaneous recovery has taken place, may show macrocytosis.

In the strict vegetarian (vegan) the macrocytosis is the result of B_{12}

deficiency and is associated with severe megaloblastosis. In hypopituitarism the anaemia is usually normochromic and normocytic due to reduced marrow erythroid activity.

160. Monoclonal gammopathy   Answers: CD

Paraproteins (monoclonal protein bands) are not normally seen in acute leukaemia (either ALL or AML) or in chronic myeloid leukaemia.

In CLL both complete or incomplete monoclonal paraproteins may occur as either IgG or IgM. CLL with an IgM paraprotein may be related to Waldenstrom's disease where high levels of IgM may result in hyperviscosity. In cold haemagglutinin disease (CHAD) up to 50% of cases are associated with an underlying lymphoproliferative disease producing an IgM paraprotein. Chad is also seen with mycoplasma pneumonia. In paroxysmal cold haemaglobinuria Donath–Landsteiner (IgG) antibodies are formed either spontaneously or as a complication of syphilis or viral infections.

The incidence of benign monoclonal gammopathy rises with age, in one large study it was 3% in people over the age of 70 years. A few may progress to multiple myeloma but the vast majority do not have increased plasma cells in the bone marrow, depression of other immunoglobulins or high levels of the monoclonal gammoglobulin.

161. Glucose-6 phosphate dehydrogenase deficiency   Answers: ABCE

G6PD deficiency is a sex-linked disorder (the affected gene being carried on the X chromosome) and is fully expressed in males. The heterozygous carrier females show a variable degree of clinical expression of the disorder.

The ingestion of oxidant drugs (e.g. anti-malarials, sulphonamides, nitrofurantoin, dapsone, probenecid, etc.) may result in an acute haemolytic episode due to the effect of the drug on intrinsically abnormal red cells that are unable to maintain normal glutathione levels. Most often haemolytic episodes are triggered by bacterial or viral infection. In Mediterranean types exposure to fava beans can precipitate a crisis.

Neonatal jaundice due to G6PD deficiency (non drug induced) is quite common in certain Mediterranean, Middle Eastern and Far Eastern countries.

Haemolysis associated with G6PD deficiency is characteristically non-spherocytic.

Mild forms of G6PD deficiency are particularly common amongst North and Central American negroes where drug-induced haemolysis tends to occur. More severe types (with chronic haemolytic anaemia) are seen in the Mediterranean countries (including areas of the Middle East), Far Eastern communities and also in Sephardic and Kurdish Jews.

162. Sickle cell anaemia   Answers: ADE

Folic acid deficiency may increase aplastic crises and folate supplements are recommended, particularly during pregnancy when crisis frequency may increase.

Chronic haemolysis results in very low or absent haptoglobins, while serum iron levels are normal or raised. The blood picture is of marked anaemia, low packed cell volume (20–25%) with polychromasia, target cells and reticulocytosis.

Recurrent infarcts lead to splenic fibrosis and shrinkage, pulmonary hypertension and focal neurological signs. Recurrent haematuria, occasionally nephrotic syndrome, aseptic femoral head necrosis and priapism may all occur.

Septic complications are most frequent and life threatening. At any age metastatic abscess formation due to *Salmonella* infection may occur.

Pneumococcal septicaemia is a a major hazard because of hyposplenism. Prophylactic penicillin and vaccination are used.

INFECTIOUS AND TROPICAL DISEASES

163. Infective diarrhoeal illness
Answer: B

In adults, pathogenic bacteria, particularly *Salmonella* and *Campylobacter,* account for up to 50% of culture positive hospitalised cases.

Clostridium difficile toxin diarrhoea is associated with antibiotic usage in about 50% and oral vancomycin or metronidazole is useful in symptomatic cases.

Generally, antimicrobials are not indicated in the treatment of acute infectious diarrhoea since, for example, ampicillin may prolong the carriage rate in salmonellosis. However, erythromycin rapidly eradicates *Campylobacter* and probably reduces the duration of abdominal pain.

It is not uncommon for several organisms to produce a colitis which may be indistinguishable from ulcerative colitis or Crohn's disease.

Cholera vaccination gives only a 50% protection rate for a maximum of 6 months. It is associated with a significant prevalence of side-effects and is usually not indicated for the occasional traveller.

164. Toxic shock syndrome (TSS)
Answers: ACD

Hypotension (which is often refractory) together with an erythematous and later desquamating rash are absolute criteria. Although initially it was described in association with tampons of the hyperabsorbent type, their withdrawal from the market has only been associated with a moderate fall in prevalence. TSS occurs in males and also in non-menstruating females, so the epidemiological spectrum is broad.

The cause is an enterotoxin produced by *Staphylococcus aureus.* Severe myalgic involvement occurs in many individuals, producing an elevated CPK.

In menstruating females, especially those who did not receive initial appropriate staphylococcal antibiotics, recurrence can be a problem.

Treatment should be with a beta-lactamase resistant penicillin such as flucloxacillin because the *Staph. aureus* is phage type 29 and 52, which is penicillinase producing.

165. Typhoid fever   Answers: BCE

Rose spots are highly suggestive, but not pathognomonic, because a similar rash occurs in paratyphoid, *Shigella, E. coli*, other Gram-negative infections, meningococcaemia and psittacosis.

Biochemical hepatitis is common because of the multi-systemic nature of the disease.

Amoxicillin is as effective as chloramphenicol and, is probably superior in terms of fever duration and relapse rate.

Formerly, intestinal perforation was managed medically, but the mortality rate has been shown to be diminished by early aggressive laparotomy.

Focal neurological signs do occur. Toxic confusion and apathy are very common. Convulsions, cerebellar ataxia and hemiplegia are seen occasionally.

166. Epstein–Barr virus   Answers: BCDE

Both the Epstein–Barr (EBV) and cytomegalovirus (CMV) can cause infectious mononucleosis after a blood transfusion, but CMV is the commoner.

B-lymphocytes become immortalised by the EBV genome, most of the DNA lying free as episomal DNA.

Although in the majority of cases EBV infections are self-limiting and benign, occasional overwhelming infections occur in individuals who have the X-linked recessive immune deficiency syndrome (the Duncan syndrome). It is thought to be due to disordered immunoregulation due to anomalous killer cells.

Antimicrobials do not alter the course of the illness. Steroids, however, may prove life-saving in upper respiratory tract obstruction. They are also useful for autoimmune phenomena or thrombocytopenia.

If ampicillin is given, the rash can be very severe, occurring in as many as 90% of patients and is thought to be due to ampicillin antibodies.

167. Meningococcal meningitis   Answers: DE

Of the 400 cases notified annually to the Communicable Diseases Surveillance Centre, Group B accounts for 60% and Group C 30%. This has implications for vaccine prophylaxis because of poor immunogenicity to Group B polysaccharide vaccine.

The Waterhouse–Friderichsen syndrome with acute adrenal failure is rare and cortisol levels in acute meningococcaemia are usually elevated.

A delay in instituting effective therapy is an 'avoidable mortality factor' and lumbar puncture should be deferred until after antibiotic administration.

The clinical diagnosis is supported by a characteristic CSF polymorph pleocytosis, low glucose, antigen detection (by counter current immune electrophoresis) and low CSF lactate.

Two days of rifampicin given to all household contacts is effective in reducing the rate of transmission one thousand fold.

168. Acquired immune deficiency syndrome   Answers: ABCDE

Opportunistic infections indicate a greater degree of immune-incompetence and *Pneumocystis carinii* infection is associated with a worse prognosis than Kaposi's sarcoma.

Due to their highly atopic status, a rash occurs in about a third of those given cotrimoxazole for definitive treatment of *Pneumocystis carinii* pneumonia. This is probably due to the sulphonamide component and these patients can be desensitised. Alternatively pentamidine can be used.

Thrombocytopenia is a good 'soft marker' of AIDS. Often it is asymptomatic and may resolve spontaneously but a few only respond to high dose human normal immunoglobulin (HNIB, used in passive prophylaxis of rubella, measles and hepatitis A) or splenectomy.

Toxoplasmosis not only produces lymphadenopathy and chorioretinitis, but sometimes intracerebral mass lesions without focal neurological signs.

169. Lassa fever   Answers: BDE

The incubation period of Lassa fever is between 7 and 21 days and should be considered as part of the differential diagnosis in those returning from Central Africa within 3 weeks with a fever.

The rodent vector is *Mastomys natalensis* and the mode of spread is via aerosols of its urine.

Haemorrhagic manifestations are usually due to abnormal coagulation rather than thrombocytopenia. The common mode of onset is insidious and non-specific symptoms. Subsequently symptoms of a systemic viral infection are manifest with headache, myalgia and pharyngitis. Other signs are non-tender lymphadenopathy, intractable vomiting and lower abdominal pain. In the second week, widespread oedema is common with haemorrhage. Hypotension is often found with an initial relative bradycardia. Fatality is up to 25% with the index cases having the higest rate. (Person to person nosocomial infection occurs.)

170. Legionnaires' disease   Answers: BE

Legionnaires' disease (usually due to *Legionella pneumophila* serotype 1) accounts for up to almost a quarter of all cases of community acquired pneumonia, but differentiation clinically from other types of pneumonia is not possible. The incidence of diarrhoea, for example, is similar in legionnellosis, pneumococcal pneumonia and mycoplasma pneumonia. However, cerebellar ataxia, peripheral neuropathy and poor memory are recognised neurological complications, possibly mediated by a cerebral toxin.

Male sex (often middle age), smoking, high alcohol consumption, pre-existing immunocompromisation (e.g. malignancy, renal disease) and chronic airflow obstruction increase the risk of acquiring legionnellosis.

Only erythromycin given for 3 weeks is effective in reducing the mortality rate. Rifampicin given alone increases resistance.

Pontiac fever (legionnellosis without pneumonia) is a 'flu-like' illness which differs from Legionnaires' disease in its higher attack rate, lower median age, shorter duration, epidemic tendency, no association with underlying disease, and a zero mortality.

171. Tuberculous meningitis   Answers: BE

Tuberculous meningitis is an uncommon cause of meningitis in the UK, but is the most common cause worldwide of subacute meningitis in non-AIDS patients. About 3–10% of all cases of tuberculosis have meningitis.

The typical CSF shows many white cells – usually 100–400/mm^3 – which are predominantly or exclusively lymphocytes, a very high protein (e.g. >1.0 g/l) and a low glucose. This picture is characteristic and clinically useful as acid fast bacilli are seen in the CSF in only a minority of cases and culture is positive in only 25–50%. Thus, confirmation of the diagnosis is difficult.

Treatment for tuberculous meningitis and tuberculomas is similar to that for other forms of tuberculosis with two exceptions:

- Four drugs should be given initially rather than three as this disease has such a poor outlook if undertreated. Resistance is an increasing problem in *M. tuberculosis*;
- Dexamethasone should be used.

The mortality of tuberculous meningitis is about 15–50%, depending on the delay in treatment. Neurological sequelae, such as diplopia, deafness, hemiparesis and mental retardation are common in survivors (20–25%). A significant proportion of patients (10–20%) develop hydrocephalus (headache or declining mental status) and require a ventricular shunt.

172. Acute osteomyelitis   Answers: CE

Acute osteomyelitis may follow a bacteraemic episode usually with *S. aureus*, but occasionally with Gram-positive, Gram-negative (e.g. *Salmonella*) or anaerobic bacteria. The most common site is the vertebral column, but no bone in the body is exempt.

The patient almost always has fever and localised pain that is persistent (palpation is painful). Sometimes patients are very ill when bacteraemia develops and do not complain of pain. Often the osteomyelitis presents days or weeks after the bacteraemic episode.

There may be a raised white cell count and the ESR or C-reactive protein is almost always extremely high. Blood cultures are often positive for *S. aureus*. Plain radiographs of the affected areas are normal for at least the first 10 days and may then show bone destruction. Bone scan and white cell scans show abnormalities of the affected area earlier than radiographs.

The principles of management are:

- Establish the extent of infection by radiology and isotope scanning of the affected site

- Ascertain the bacterial cause using direct needle puncture under radiographic control

- Intravenous antibiotic therapy with large antibiotic doses as bony penetration is relatively poor

- Immobilisation of the area, particularly if a critical part of the vertebral column is involved or there is evidence of epidural compression

- Review by an orthopaedic surgeon. If there is extensive involvement or localised abscess formation impinging on important structures such as the spinal cord, surgery is often mandatory.

173. ^{111}Indium leucocyte scanning   Answers: ACDE

The technique of labelling leucocytes extracorporeally and then reinjecting them is used to localise areas of sepsis, often at unknown sites. Donor white cells may be used in the neutropenic patient.

Some abscesses can be identified within 30 minutes of the reinjection, but the maximum sensitivity is not reached for 24 hours. The cells are also taken up by the reticuloendothelial system in the bone marrow, liver, and spleen.

False positive scans occur with haematomas and inflammatory disease, and false negatives with chronic sepsis.

174. Hepatitis B vaccine   Answer: AD

About 200 million people are thought to be carriers of hepatitis B virus. The rate for different parts of the world varies from 15–30% in the Far East to 5% in Southern Europe and 0.1% in Britain.

The infectivity of the blood depends on the antigens and antibodies present. If the 'e' antigen is present then there is active replication and the serum is highly infectious. The presence of the antibody to this antigen alone implies a lower risk. Serum that is hepatitis B surface antigen (HBSAg) positive is intermediate between the two states.

In babies born to carrier mothers both the immunoglobulin (passive immunisation) and the vaccine should be given at delivery to afford maximum protection.

175. Human prion disease   Answers: AC

Prion comes from the term **pro**teinacious **in**fectious particle. They are small infectious pathogens containing protein, which resist procedures that destroy nucleic acids (e.g. UV light).

Human prion diseases are transmissible neurodegenerative disorders (TNDs). These are chronic, progressive CNS illnesses, which include Kuru and Creutzfeldt–Jakob in humans along with scrapie and BSE in animals.

The disease is confined to the CNS and is characterised by a long incubation period and 100% mortality. Histologically, there is reactive astrocytosis with little inflammatory reaction and small vacuoles (spongiform change).

Prion disease can be transmitted by inoculation of tissue into CNS. The abnormal prion protein has been found to be produced by a gene on chromosome 20 that normally produces a similar harmless protein. It is thought that the abnormal prion triggers its own manufacture by the host.

176. HIV infection   **Answers: ACDE**

Interleukin 2 is produced by CD4 cells and so is impaired. Polyclonal B cell activation is stimulated. The virus encodes a protein which acts as a superantigen that binds abnormally between macrophages and CD4 cells.

HIV infection causes increases in several acute phase proteins including β_2 microglobulin. Expression of CD receptors makes cells prone to infection – predominantly CD4+ lymphocytes but also moncytes/macrophages, dendritic cells, megakaryocytes and astrocytes.

RHEUMATOLOGY

177. Vasculitis   Answers: ABC

Cranial arteritis (also called giant cell, temporal arteritis) is a medium and large vessel arteritis. There is a strong association with polymyalgia rheumatica. It is very rare under the age of 55.

Polyarteritis nodosa is an arteritis of medium and small arteries. A necrotising proliferative glomerulonephritis with crescent formation is commonly found at autopsy. Progressive renal failure and hypertension are the most common causes of death. The histological features of polyarteritis nodosa are fibrinoid necrosis and cellular infiltrates. All three layers of the arterial wall are involved. Vascular granulomata characterise Wegener's granulomatosis.

The kidneys are rarely affected clinically in rheumatoid arthritis, although histological changes may be found on biopsy. Small arteries are usually involved, resulting in cutaneous ulcers, neuropathy and digital infarcts.

Waldenstrom's macroglobulinaemia is a lymphoproliferative disorder producing macroglobulin proteins with consequent hyperviscosity. No associated vasculitis is described.

178. Osteoporosis   Answers: BC

Osteoid mineralisation is normal in osteoporosis, but impaired in osteomalacia. Osteoporosis is the result of reduction of the total mass of normally mineralised bone.

Causes of secondary osteoporosis include corticosteroid therapy, Cushing's syndrome, rheumatoid arthritis, hypogonadism, subtotal gastrectomy, immobilisation, renal failure, thyrotoxicosis and hyperparathyroidism.

Vertebral collapse due to osteoporosis may result in nerve root compression, whereas cord compression is rare. Common manifestations are fractures, particularly neck of femur and Colles.

Calcitonin acts on bone to reduce the rate of bone resorption and hence opposes the effect of osteoporosis. Postmenopausal oestrogen replacement is the most effective in preserving bone mass in at-risk women. In patients with vertebral collapse, biphosphonates can prevent further crush fractures.

Hydroxyproline is produced from bone collagen and is raised when bone turnover is increased. It is often elevated in Paget's disease and hyperparathyroidism, and is either normal or raised in osteoporosis.

179. Synovial fluid   Answer: B

The synovial fluid is produced by the synovium, and removed by phagocytic cells and lymphatic drainage. The synovium lies within the joint capsule. In normal joints, the synovial fluid viscosity is high. In inflammatory arthritis the normal synovial constituents are altered, effectively reducing the viscosity.

The synovial membrane in rheumatoid arthritis is infiltrated by lymphocytes and plasma cells, but paradoxically the synovial fluid typically contains polymorphonuclear cells attracted by chemotactic factors.

Uric acid crystals (gout) are negatively birefringent under a polarising light microscope. Pyrophosphate crystals (pseudogout) are weakly positively birefringent.

Bloodstaining of synovial fluid is commonly due to trauma or bleeding disorders. Pseudogout, septic arthritis and Charcot's joints may also produce bloodstained fluid. Tumours (e.g. villonodular synovitis) are relatively rare.

180. Rheumatoid arthritis   Answers: BDE

The Rose Waaler and latex agglutination tests detect IgM rheumatoid factor. IgG rheumatoid factor is less common and can only be measured by techniques such as radio immunoassay.

The presence of rheumatoid nodules is almost always associated with seropositivity. Felty's syndrome and Sjögren's disease are also more common in seropositive patients.

Amyloidosis in rheumatoid arthritis usually presents as proteinuria or, if severe, the nephrotic syndrome. Felty's syndrome causes splenomegaly, leg ulceration and leucopenia and possibly pancytopenia in rheumatoid arthritis.

Dry eyes (keratoconjunctivitis sicca) and dry mouth are features of Sjögren's syndrome, which can be primary, or secondary to rheumatoid arthritis (in which almost 100% are seropositive), SLE, scleroderma, mixed connective tissue disease, dermatomyositis and occasionally fibrosing alveolitis or liver disease. ANA and Ro (SS-A) antibodies are more often positive in primary Sjögrens syndrome.

Thrombocytosis is characteristic of active rheumatoid arthritis. ESR, plasma viscosity and C-reactive protein often, but not always, reflect disease activity.

181. Polymyositis   Answers: BC

In children, polymyositis is not associated with malignancy and it often has vasculitic complications. In adults, cancers of lung, ovary, breast and stomach are associated but still only occur in less than 10% of cases. Older men and those with dermatomyositis are the highest risk groups.

The clinical picture is usually of insidious onset with predominantly proximal muscle weakness. Half the patients complain of pain and tenderness. General malaise and weight loss are common. The characteristic heliotrope rash occurs in up to 40% with a further 20% having an atypical rash.

The electromyographic features of polymyositis are

- Polyphasic motor unit potential
- Spontaneous fibrillation and positive sharp waves
- Bizarre high frequency repetitive discharges

Biopsies are occasionally negative, because of patchy muscle involvement. If muscles are too atrophic, biopsy may be unhelpful in distinguishing polymyositis from other muscle diseases.

182. Scleroderma   Answer: E

Scleroderma typically presents in the 4th to the 6th decade with swelling and stiffness of fingers preceded by Raynaud's phenomenon for several months or years. The cause of the condition is unknown. The histopathological sequence is: (a) inflammation; ((b) fibrosis; and (c) atrophy. There is also concentric proliferation and thickening of the intima within the vascular bed. The pattern of organ involvement varies, but occasionally the changes are localised to a patch of skin (morphoea).

In the skin, the disease starts with painless oedema, followed by thickening of the fingers, hands and face – sometimes more widely. As atrophy develops, the face becomes 'pinched', with a beaked nose, small mouth (microstomia) and widespread telangiectasiae. There is also alopecia, pigmentation and vitiligo. Subcutaneous calcification occurs in nodules, particularly around the finger tips and these may ulcerate.

The second commonest system affected is the gastrointestinal tract. In the oesophagus, there is decreased/absent peristalsis with dilatation. Patients may be asymptomatic or may have marked dysphagia and heartburn. In the small bowel, stasis and dilatation occurs with bacterial overgrowth and malabsorption.

In the musculoskeletal system, there are flexion and spindling deformities of the fingers. Other problems are myositis and myocardial fibrosis (conduction defects and arrhythmias). The lungs may show fibrosis and honeycombing leading to a restrictive defect. Sjögrens sydrome may be present.

The most serious problems are progressive renal failure and malignant hypertension due to an obliterative endarteritis. There is no treatment. Control of blood pressure is important and oesophageal problems are managed symptomatically. Around half of patients will survive 5 years.

A positive speckled or nucleolar antinuclear antibody is present in the majority of patients and rheumatoid factor is found in up to one-third. Many have a normochromic normocytic anaemia with a raised ESR.

A benign variant of systemic sclerosis is known by the acronym CREST: *C*alcinosis, *R*aynaud's, *E*sophagitis, *S*clerodactyly and *T*elangectasia. Anticentromere antibodies are specific to this condition (now termed *limited cutaneous scleroderma*).

183. Infectious arthropathies   Answers: ABDE

Gonococcal arthritis often presents as an acute migratory polyarthritis affecting upper and lower limbs. There is often an associated skin rash and fever. Response to therapy is usually rapid.

Viral infections may precipitate an inflammatory polyarthritis. It is usually immune complex mediated, although in rubella the virus can occasionally be recovered from the synovial fluid. Hepatitis, mumps and parvovirus have been implicated.

Tuberculous septic arthritis is often insidious. The diagnosis is best made by synovial biopsy and recognition of typical caseating granulomata. The organism is only rarely found in the synovial fluid.

Reiter's syndrome is typically a triad of conjunctivitis, urethritis and arthritis. It is precipitated by an attack of dysentery or non-specific urethritis. Keratoderma blenorrhagica and circinate balanitis are complications of Reiter's disease.

184. Histocompatibility antigens (HLA)   Answers: BCD

The major histocompatibility complex of man is found on the short arm of chromosome 6. The haplotype for any one individual is determined at conception and does not change through life. HLA antigens are present on all cells except trophoblasts and mature erythrocytes.

Patients with HLA B27 who acquire dysentery have a greater risk than others of developing Reiter's syndrome. This may be due to cross reaction of cell surface antigens.

HLA DR4 and HLA DW4 are associated with seropositive rheumatoid arthritis; HLA DR2 and HLA DR3 with systemic lupus erythematosus.

HLA B27 status is associated with a nearly 500 fold increased risk of ankylosing spondylitis. However, not all patients with ankylosing spondylitis are HLA B27 positive and the diagnosis should be made on clinical and radiological grounds.

185. Joint involvement   Answers: BCE

In rheumatoid arthritis there is typically a symmetrical polyarthritis affecting the metacarpophalangeal and proximal interphalangeal joints in the hand. Almost all joints may be involved, but the DIP joints are typically spared.

In osteoarthritis DIP (Heberden's nodes) and first CMC joints are commonly affected. Hip, knee and first MTP joints are also prone to osteoarthritis.

Pseudogout can affect more than one joint at a time. The most common joints involved are the wrist and knee. These are also involved in chronic pyrophosphate arthropathy.

Systemic lupus erythematosus affects MCP, PIP, wrists and knees symmetrically. Radiologically the arthritis differs from rheumatoid arthritis in the absence of erosions. Sacroiliitis is a feature of ankylosing spondylitis and Reiter's disease.

Diffuse idiopathic skeletal hyperostosis (Forrestier's disease) is a disease characterised by bony overgrowth of osteophytes, typically causing bony fusion of the vertebrae, commencing at the thoracolumbar junction. Associated hypertrophic osteoarthritis of peripheral joints is a common feature.

186. Gout   Answers: ACE

Monosodium urate monohydrate crystals (negatively birefringent) are precipitated in connective tissue in the presence of hyperuricaemia. Their presence can be (i) asymptomatic, (ii) associated with attacks of gout, (iii) associated with tophi.

The purine residues of nucleic acids are metabolised via hypoxanthine and xanthine to uric acid by xanthine oxidase. Care must be taken when starting patients on allopurinol (a xanthine oxidase inhibitor) as acute attacks can be precipitated. A non-steroidal anti-inflammatory drug or low dose colchicine can be used to cover the first few months of treatment.

High dose aspirin is uricosuric, whereas low dose aspirin causes hyperuricaemia by its effect on renal tubule function (prevents distal tubular secretion). Other uricosuric drugs are probenecid and sulphinpyrazone (no dose effect).

Calcium pyrophosphate dihydrate (CPPD) crystals are found in synovial fluid in pseudogout attacks. Radiologically CPPD deposition may appear as chondrocalcinosis.

187. Therapy of connective tissue diseases   Answers: ABDE

Both gold and D-penicillamine can cause an immune complex membranous glomerulopathy with proteinuria or even nephrotic syndrome. Recovery may take 12–18 months after stopping treatment.

The mechanism of action of D-penicillamine in rheumatoid arthritis is not clear. It does not appear to be related to its ability to chelate divalent cations, and it has no cytotoxic or anti-inflammatory properties.

Amyloid nephropathy is associated with longstanding rheumatoid arthritis *per se*. Differentiation from drug-induced nephropathy may be made by renal biopsy (Congo red stain).

Glaucoma, cataract and benign intracranial hypertension are much more common in the iatrogenic form of Cushing's syndrome probably related to the length of exposure to excess corticosteroids (cf. symptoms in ectopic production of ACTH).

Hydroxychloroquine can cause reversible diplopia and corneal deposits. The retinopathy is more serious as it can be irreversible.

Low dose prednisolone improves the long term outlook of rheumatoid disease.

188. Systemic lupus erythematosus (SLE)   Answers: AE

Antinuclear antibodies are present in about 95% patients with SLE, but are not specific. Anti double stranded DNA antibodies and anti Sm (a soluble nuclear Ag) are highly specific to SLE. Antibodies to the cytoplasmic protein Ro (SSA) and La (SSB) are also associated with SLE, but are less specific.

Slow acetylators are more prone to drug-induced lupus than normal acetylators. Drugs that are incriminated in SLE include hydralazine, procainamide and isoniazid. Drug-induced lupus is associated with antibodies to single stranded DNA.

Renal involvement (due to a glomerulonephritis) is apparent in about half of patients with SLE and is characterised by mild to moderate proteinuria, microscopic haematuria and casts. Nephrotic syndrome and renal insufficiency occur less frequently.

Hypocomplementaemia (particularly C3, C4) occurs in active disease, and is probably related to complement activation by immune complexes. Such deposits are commonly found in skin and kidney at biopsy. Reduction of the lymphocyte count often reflects disease activity. The neutrophil count is usually within normal limits.

IMMUNOLOGY

189. Placental transfer   Answers: ACE

Of the immunoglobulins only IgG class is selectively transferred across the placenta. IgA and the higher molecular weight IgM are excluded. Thus IgM antibodies in the newborn are of fetal origin and indicate a response to intrauterine infection.

Unconjugated bilirubin is rapidly transferred from fetus to mother by active transport whereas conjugated bilirubin crosses only slowly.

Heparin does not cross the placenta, making its use in pregnancy preferable to warfarin, which passes to the fetal circulation and may result in fetal/ neonatal haemorrhage or congenital malformation.

Thyroid stimulating immunoglobulin is of IgG class and in maternal Graves' disease can cross the placenta and cause transient neonatal thyrotoxicosis.

190. Selective IgA deficiency   Answers: AE

This is the commonest primary immune defect, with a prevalence of about 1 in 700 in the UK.

IgG2 and IgG4 subclass deficiencies are those usually associated with selective IgA deficiency and may lead to recurrent infections (particularly organisms with polysaccharide antigens). Deficiencies of IgG1 and IgG3 similarly occur together, but pre-dispose to different infections (protein antigens).

Salivary IgA is normally completely absent (gut humoral immunity is maintained by substituting IgM instead). Coeliac disease SLE and rheumatoid disease are associated with selective IgA deficiency.

191. Anti-neutrophil cytoplasmic antibodies (ANCA)   Answers: ABD

There are two common types: cytoplasmic (c) ANCA, which is associated with Wegener's granulomatosis, and has specificity usually for a neutrophil serine protease; and perinuclear (p) ANCA, associated with a variety of other vasculitides (polyarteritis nodosa, microscopic polyarteritis, SLE), which has specificity for myeloperoxidase.

The serum antibodies are helpful in diagnosis, but may become undetectable soon after treatment.

192. The lupus anticoagulant   Answers: BCDE

The lupus anticoagulant is one of the antiphospholipid antibodies, which are usually IgG or IgM. In SLE. It is associated with fetal loss and recurrent arterial and venous thromboses. It is probable that placental infarcts are the cause of increased fetal loss. The effect is due to IgG antibodies (IgM antibodies are less significant) that affect the lipid-soluble clotting factors and prolong the kaolin-cephalin clotting time (KCCT), which does not correct with the addition of normal plasma factor (because the IgG blocks the fresh factors).

Fetal loss can be reduced by low dose aspirin and, in those with a previous history, heparin.

The primary syndrome is associated with thrombocytopenia. Thrombotic episodes are reduced by anticoagulation with warfarin.

193. The Ro (SS-A) Extractable Nuclear Antigen antibody   ABDE

The antibody is found early in lupus, sometimes before antinuclear antibodies.

Livedo reticularis is one of the skin signs in lupus (also in primary antiphospholipid antibody syndrome and polyarteritis nodosa).

In systemic sclerosis the specific antibody (against topoisomerase-l) is Scl 70. Many other ENA specificities may occur.

194. Immunoglobulin G subclass 2   Answers: AC

IgG2 deficiency may occur in symptomatic IgA deficient patients and is associated with recurrent sino-pulmonary infections and otitis media.

Unlike IgG1 and IgG3 (which develop in the first year), IgG2 develops more slowly over the first two years of life and adult levels of IgG2 (and IgG4) are only achieved later.

IgG4 is the subclass seen in 'allergic' conditions, together with IgE.

The immunoglobulins fix complement via the the 'classical' (C 142) rather than the alternate (properdin/factor B) pathway.

195. AIDS   **Answers: All False**

The best available marker of disease progression is the absolute count of (CD4+) cells, (not the CD4:CD8 ratio which can be affected by infection, and the viral load). 99% of the virus found in the plasma is derived from infected CD4 cells particularly in lymphoid tissue. Up to 2 billion CD4 cells may by destroyed and replaced daily. When the body's ability to do this fails, the counts fall and clinical immunodeficiency occur.

There are many new products coming on to the market. The evidence is that combination therapy is superior with fewer side-effects. Triple therapy may eradicate the virus.

HIV1 is far commoner throughout Europe. HIV2 is found particularly in Africa.

Treatment is currently recommended when plasma HIV RNA values exceed 5,000–30,000 copies/ml; or when CD4 count is less than 500 cells x 10^6/l; or with the onset of symptoms.

Haemophiliacs can infect their wives by unprotected intercourse, and require advice and counselling.

Monocytes and other antigen-presenting cells (and gut cells) carry the CD4 surface antigen and can be infected by HIV.

STATISTICS

196. Confidence limits   Answers: BCDE

The recommendations of the major scientific journals are that confidence limits should be calculated and shown for all results. The reasons for this involve considerations of the errors which can occur in analysing a trial.

A type I error is a false-positive result where if $p = 0.10$ the result will occur by chance in one in ten trials. If $p = 0.50$ then it may happen in every other trial. Thus even at $p < 0.01$ the result may be falsely interpreted as being of significance.

A type II error is a false-negative assumption. Thus at $p = 0.20$ it is possible that the treatments were significantly different. The probability of detecting differences can be calculated for any trial given the number involved in the trial. This gives a measure of its power to discern a significant result. The wider the difference between treatments, the less chance a type II error will be made.

The confidence limits are related to type II errors, and are important when the differences between treatments are small and there are few participants in a trial. The higher the number of participants, the narrower the 95% confidence band will be. Hence 95% limits (based on the sample mean and standard deviation) indicate that there is only a 5% chance of the true population mean lying outside these.

197. Chi-squared test   Answers: BCE

The chi-squared test is a non-parametric test (data grouped by category) which is always carried out on absolute numbers not proportions, means or percentages. The method is to construct a table of the data, then for each cell the expected number is calculated. The difference between the observed and expected is recorded, the result squared and divided by the expected number [$(O-E)^2/E$]; the chi-squared statistic is the sum of all the values (Σ).

The degree of freedom is (number of rows – 1) x (number of columns – 1).

In the chi-squared test the expected value in any one cell should not be less than 5. Yates' correction overcomes this to some degree.

Potential confounding variables occur where there is some factor, other than the one you are testing, influencing the result.

198. Correlation coefficient   Answer: B

A correlation coefficient is a measure of a linear relationship between two independently measured variables. A value of 1.0 indicates a perfect positive relationship, –1.0 a negative one and zero the absence of a linear one. It is possible that in a 'U' shaped relationship (quadratic) then the correlation could be zero.

It is a Pearson correlation coefficient that is calculated for two variables on an interval scale. For those on an ordinal scale a Spearman rank correlation coefficient is calculated.

The p value depends on the correlation found and the number studied, thus in large scale epidemiological studies a value of 0.3 could be statistically significant.

199. Standard deviation   Answers: BCD

There are a number of different types of data. Nominal is categorical data. Ordinal implies a scale of effect but not the magnitude of change. An interval scale implies a constant known relationship when moving from point to point.

The standard deviation is a measure of the scatter of observations about the mean, it is less distorted by extreme values when compared to the range. Standard deviation is the square root of the variance.

The standard error is a measure of the accuracy of the sample mean when compared with the unknown population mean. It is calculated by $SD/\sqrt{N}$ where N is the number in the sample.

200. General statistics   Answers: BCD

$p = 0.001$ means that the result could have occured by chance at 1 in a 100 observations, $p = 0.05$ occurs in 1 in 20 observations. The former is of greater statistical significance.

Prevalence is the total number of cases (old and new) at a certain point in time. The incidence is the number of new cases occurring over a set period. In a chronic condition prevalence >> incidence. In a short-lived condition, such as measles, prevalence can equal incidence.

The mean is the average value, the mode the most frequently occurring value and the median that which divides the values by half (in a continuous distribution it divides the areas under the curve equally).

201. Gaussian distribution   **Answers: ABC**

Two standard deviations from the mean is approximately at a $p = 0.05$ (actually 1.96 SD) probability, 2.6 SD is at $p = 0.01$.

A Poisson distribution is discrete and relates to the number of events which happen in a fixed time interval. It can be used, for example, to compare death rates that can be regarded as happening by random event in a community.

The binomial distribution is also discrete (i.e. an event happens or not). It describes the distribution which occurs when considering the number of successes in 'n' independent trials where the probability of one trial being a success is p.

DERMATOLOGY

202. Granuloma annulare   Answers: CDE

Granuloma annulare is a disease of unknown aetiology which often starts in a single area but may develop into multiple lesions. It is usually confined to the extremities and is painless. The disease may persist for many years and there is no effective treatment.

There is a probable association with diabetes mellitus.

Histologically, there is collagen necrobiosis which is also seen in necrobiosis lipoidica diabeticorum and rheumatoid nodules.

The appearances of a hard raised edge and the absence of scaling and pruritus distinguish it from a fungal infection.

203. Pyoderma gangrenosum   Answers: ABCE

Pyoderma gangrenosum is typically an irregular ulcer appearing on the lower limb with a violacious colour, cribiform scarring and undermined edge.

Biopsy of the ulcer does not show any pathognomonic features. The aetiology is unclear but recent work has demonstrated an immune vasculitis.

It is associated with a seronegative arthritis (not necessarily linked to bowel disease), paraproteinaemias (malignant and benign) and inflammatory bowel disease. The ulcer often develops at the site of minor trauma.

The relationship to inflammatory bowel disease is complex. It may predate any gastrointestinal problems, but, if severe, the skin lesion will often heal after a panproctocolectomy. Occasionally pyoderma gangrenosum appears after a colectomy.

High dose steroids are effective in healing the ulcers.

204. Urticaria   Answers: ABCDE

Urticaria or angioedema affects approximately 15% of the population at some time. Episodes are termed chronic if lasting for more than 2 months.

The rare syndrome of hereditary angioedema due to C1 esterase inhibitor deficiency needs to be excluded where respiratory or gastrointestinal features are present. Treatment is by donor serum if an attack is severe. Prophylactic management involves the use of stanazol or danazol. Tranexamic acid is occasionally employed.

Precipitating factors are multiple:

- Physical agents, e.g. cold, heat, exercise
- Drugs, salicylates and other NSAIDs, codeine or other opiates
- Food additives, benzoic acid, preservatives, tartrazine
- Viral or parasitic infections, especially in children.

H_1 antihistamines are the mainstay of treatment, they are more effective against the itching than the swelling. In severe cases a short course of oral corticosteroids may be required. Acute airway obstruction is treated by adrenaline (parenteral or inhaled).

205. Lichen planus   Answers: ACD

In the 'classical' cases of lichen planus, flat topped, shiny, purplish, pruritic, polygonal papules are seen anywhere on the body, but with a predeliction for the wrists, lower back and the ankles. They are often surmounted by a whitish lacy pattern (Wickham's striae). Koebner's phenomenon is also observed where papules appear at the sites of minor trauma including scratching. Oral lesions are found in approximately 70% of cases.

Other manifestations include:

- Isolated involvement of the mouth and genitalia (which, if chronic, may ulcerate and are pre-malignant)
- Herpes zoster like lesions
- Scarring alopecia
- Severe nail damage.

Occasionally severe hypertrophic areas develop, and in coloured patients hyperpigmentation may be found.

Typically, there is acute onset followed by spontaneous clearing, but in some patients it may persist indefinitely.

The histopathology is characteristic with liquefactive degeneration of the basal layer of the epidermis in a 'saw tooth' pattern. In the dermis a band of T-lymphocyte infiltration is found. Immune studies have shown IgM deposits around the colloid bodies formed in the upper dermis.

206. Skin manifestations of syphilis   Answer: C

Chancres are painless ulcers seen in primary syphiylis, which heal spontaneously within 3 months.

The typical rash of secondary syphilis starts as a macular eruption on the trunk, then becomes maculopapular and occasionally pustular as it spreads peripherally. Secondary syphilis can result in patchy alopecia due to infection of hair follicles. Moist areas of the body develop condylomata lata. Highly infectious lesions occur on mucosal surfaces. Painless lymphadenopathy is common.

Gummae involve many tissues, but typically affect the skin and skeletal tissue. Skin presentation varies from deep granulomata through to superficial nodules which may ulcerate. Spirochaetes are difficult to demonstrate in late manifestations.

MOLECULAR AND GENETIC MEDICINE

207. Polymerase chain reaction   Answers: BDE

The polymerase chain reaction (PCR) is a way of amplifying or making multiple copies of any desired nucleic acid.

RNA can be studied by making a DNA copy of the RNA using the virus enzyme reverse transcriptase. Detecting mRNA and mapping it onto a specific gene does not prove that the protein is being made.

Detecting amino acid substitutions is very useful, for example studies of the prion protein (PrP) gene can show whether an individual is susceptible to the iatrogenic form of Creutzfeld–Jakob disease or the familial form.

Viral nucleic acid may be identified when no virus can be found. One example is recovery of coxsackie virus nucleic acid from the blood of patients with insulin dependent diabetes.

208. Asthma   Answers: BE

Asthma is an inherited polygenic disorder.

Polymorphisms of the N-terminal of the β_2 adrenoceptor (gene located on chromosome 5q) are linked to severity of asthma. There are also links to the β subunit of the high affinity IgE receptor (FcϵR1 situated on chromosome 11q).

Asthma is an inflammatory disease characterised by up-regulation of a specific subclass of T helper cells (Th$_2$) in the airways leading to increased expression of Th$_2$ cytokines – interleukin 4, 5, 9. These play a crucial role in both developing and sustaining airway inflammation in response to allergen exposure.

Phospholipase C and adenylate cyclase are intra-cellular second messengers which result in a rise in cAMP and inositol 1,4,5 triphosphate. The latter causes an elevation of intracellular calcium which stimulates mediator release, cell activation or contraction depending on the cell type. Elevation of cAMP generally inhibits cell activation (e.g. relaxation of smooth muscle cells).

209. Molecular cell biology   Answer: B

Tumour necrosis factor α is a polypeptide that was initially defined as killing tumour cells in culture. It was also called cachectin because of its catabolic properties in infection and cancer. Its main role is in mobilising the acute inflammatory response.

Cell surface adhesion molecules hold cells and tissues together. Those expressed by leucocytes and endothelial cells are regulated by pro-inflammatory cytokines (i.e. increase stickiness).

Apoptosis is a precisely regulated and programmed cell death caused by the cell activating a cascade of death enzymes, which kill the cell and make it safe for clearance by phagocytes.

The extracellular matrix is composed of proteins and proteoglycans. It is very important in signalling, for example differentiation of cells (alveoli in lactating breast) or cell survival (preventing apoptosis).

A chemokine is a cytokine which attracts leucocytes. β-chemokine receptor 5 is used by HIV-1 to infect leucocytes; people with an inherited deficiency of this receptor resist invasion and may live for many years without developing AIDS.

210. Molecular biology   Answers: CD

An allele is one or more alternative forms of a gene, which occupies the same locus on a particular chromosome. Homozygotes bear identical alleles at two corresponding loci. Heterozygotes have two different alleles. There is a lot of interest in the apolipoprotein e4 allele on chromosome 19 in the development of Alzheimer's disease. It may play a part in inhibiting neuronal growth.

Positional cloning aims to identify the locus and gene responsible for the disease under scrutiny. Linkage analysis assesses the frequency with which a particular marker co-segregates with the disorder/protein in families. Because there may be crossing over of DNA between a pair of chromosomes, the further a gene is from the marker the lower the chance of co-segregation.

Transcription factors are proteins which bind promotor regions of DNA upstream of the sequences which encode mRNA, leading to assembly of RNA polymerase and transcription of the gene.

Knock-out mice have a genetic loss of function. They are created by homologous recombination and targeted mutagenesis, techniques by which the gene of interest is inactivated by swapping the normal DNA for a similar DNA construct with a mutation. Transgenic technology is used to overexpress a normal gene.

211. p53 gene   Answers: ACDE

The p53 gene is considered to be central to the development of many tumours. Its role is to prevent entry into the S phase of cell replication (DNA replication) until the genetic material has been checked and repaired.

If abnormal then the p53 gene permits the duplication of cells with abnormal genotypes. Very rare syndromes such as Li-Fraumeni predispose the person to early development of a wide range of cancers.

Somatic mutation is similarly associated with a range of tumours, including colonic carcinoma. Screening programmes for affected families are now in operation.

REVISION INDEX

Numbers shown refer to question numbers.

MORE PASTEST BOOKS FOR MRCP PART 1 CANDIDATES

MRCP PART 1 MCQ POCKET BOOKS

An exciting new range of MRCP Part 1 Pocket Books has been published to help you pass your examination. The books reflect changes to the MRCP 1 General Medicine examination, with Multiple True/False and 'Best of Five' questions. £11.95 each.

Book 1: Cardiology, Haematology, Respiratory Medicine, 2002.
ISBN 1 901198 75 8. Ref 1101.
Book 2: Basic Sciences, Neurology, Psychiatry, 2002.
ISBN 1 901198 80 4. Ref 1102.
Book 3: Endocrinology, Gastroenterology, Nephrology, 2002.
ISBN 1 901198 85 5. Ref: 1103.
Book 4: Clinical Pharmacology, Immunology, Infectious Diseases, Rheumatology, 2002.
ISBN 1 901198 90 1. Ref: 1104.

MRCP PART 1: EXPLANATIONS TO THE MRCP 1997/98 PART 1 PAPERS

PasTest has combined its two popular titles (each exam was previously published as a separate volume) into one best-selling publication.

- 360 answers and teaching notes to the recently published Royal College of Physicians book of actual exam questions
- Published by popular request and to be used alongside the Royal College publication

MRCP Part 1: Explanations to the MRCP 1997/98 Part 1 Papers, G Rees, BM BCh MD MRCP PhD 2002, ISBN 1 901198 28 6. Ref 1105. £17.95.

EXPLANATIONS TO THE ROYAL COLLEGE OF PHYSICIANS PAST PAPERS: EXPLANATIONS TO THE GREEN BOOK (1990 PAPERS)

- Answers and expert teaching notes related to the Royal College of Physicians green book of actual MRCP past exam papers.
- Indispensable revision material for all MRCP Part 1 candidates.

Explanations to the Royal College of Physicians Past Papers: Explanations to the Green Book (1990 Papers), H Beynon, MRCP & C Ross, MRCP, 1992, ISBN 0 906896 57 6. Ref: 1051. £12.95.

Credit card hotline: 01565 752000

PasTest Ltd,
FREEPOST
Knutsford
WA16 7BR

Fax: +44 (0)1565 650264
www.pastest.co.uk

PASTEST INTENSIVE COURSES FOR MRCP PART 1

PasTest is dedicated to helping doctors pass their professional examinations. We have over 25 years of specialist experience in medical education and over 4000 doctors attend our revision courses each year.

Experienced lecturers
Many of our lecturers are also examiners who teach in a lively and interesting way to ensure you:

* are familiar with current trends in exams
* receive essential advice on exam technique
* are taught how to avoid the common pitfalls

Outstanding accelerated learning
Our up-to-date comprehensive course material includes hundreds of sample questions similar to those you will experience in the exam. You will also receive detailed explanations including charts and diagrams.

Choice of courses
PasTest have a wide range of high-quality courses around the UK.

Six-day courses
* No conflict between work and study – a full week allows you to dedicate your time exclusively to study.
* All major topics covered with the time spent on each subject weighted according to the number of MCQs that typically occur in the exam.
* Four high-quality complete mock exams plus exam technique and question-spotting sessions to help you gain those vital marks.

Two consecutive weekends
* Ideal if you are not taking study leave.
* Three high-quality complete mock exams with invaluable tips on exam technique.

Refresher weekends
* Ideal if you are re-taking, need an intensive short course or to give you a taste of the exam to steer you in the right direction for revision.
* Concentrates on potential problem areas and specialties that form the core of the exam.

**For further details please contact PasTest
on Freephone 0800 980 9814**